Thomas De Quincey

De Quincey's Revolt of the Tartars

Or, flight of the Kalmuck khan and his people from the Russian territories

to the frontiers of China. Vol. 3

Thomas De Quincey

De Quincey's Revolt of the Tartars
Or, flight of the Kalmuck khan and his people from the Russian territories to the frontiers of China. Vol. 3

ISBN/EAN: 9783337149413

Printed in Europe, USA, Canada, Australia, Japan

Cover: Foto ©ninafisch / pixelio.de

More available books at **www.hansebooks.com**

THOMAS DE QUINCEY.

The Silver Series of English Classics

DE QUINCEY'S

REVOLT OF THE TARTARS

OR, FLIGHT OF THE KALMUCK KHAN AND HIS PEOPLE FROM THE RUSSIAN TERRITORIES TO THE FRONTIERS OF CHINA

EDITED WITH INTRODUCTION AND NOTES

BY

ALEXANDER S. TWOMBLY

SILVER, BURDETT AND COMPANY
NEW YORK   BOSTON   CHICAGO
1897

Norwood Press
J. S. Cushing & Co. — Berwick & Smith
Norwood Mass. U.S.A.

PUBLISHERS' ANNOUNCEMENT.

The SILVER SERIES OF ENGLISH CLASSICS is designed to furnish editions of many of the standard classics in English and American literature, in the best possible form for reading and study. While planned to meet the requirements for entrance examinations to college, as formulated by the Commission of American Colleges, it serves a no less important purpose in providing valuable and attractive reading for the use of the higher grades of public and private schools.

It is now generally recognized that to familiarize students with the masterpieces of literature is the best means of developing true literary taste, and of establishing a love of good reading which will be a permanent delight. The habit of cultured original expression is also established through the influence of such study.

To these ends, carefully edited and annotated editions of the Classics, which shall direct pupils in making intelligent and appreciative study of each work as a whole, and, specifically, of its individual features, are essential in the classroom.

The SILVER SERIES notably meets this need, through the editing of its volumes by scholars of high literary ability and educational experience. It unfolds the treasures of literary art, and shows the power and beauty of our language in the various forms of English composition, — as the oration, the essay, the argument, the biography, the poem, etc.

Thus, the first volume contains Webster's oration at the laying of the corner stone of Bunker Hill monument; and, after a brief sketch of the orator's life, the *oration* is defined, — the speech itself furnishing a practical example of what a masterpiece in oratory should be.

Next follows the *essay*, as exemplified by Macaulay's "Essay on Milton." The story of the life of the great essayist creates an interest in his work, and the student, before he proceeds to study the essay, is shown in the Introduction the difference between the oratorical and the essayistic style.

After this, Burke's "Speech on Conciliation" is treated in a similar manner, the essential principles of *forensic* authorship being set forth.

Again, De Quincey's "Flight of a Tartar Tribe" — a conspicuous example of pure *narration* — exhibits the character and quality of this department of literary composition.

Southey's "Life of Nelson" is presented in the same personal and critical manner, placing before the student the essential characteristics of the *biographical* style.

The series continues with specimens of such works as "The Rime of the Ancient Mariner," by Coleridge; the "Essay on Burns," by Carlyle; the "Sir Roger De Coverley Papers," by Addison; Milton's "Paradise Lost," Books I. and II.; Pope's "Iliad," Books I., VI., XXII., and XXIV.; Dryden's "Palamon and Arcite," and other works of equally eminent writers, covering, in the completed series, a large and diversified area of literary exposition.

The functions of the several departments of authorship are explained in simple terms. The beginner, as well as the somewhat advanced scholar, will find in this series ample instruction and guidance for his own study, without being perplexed by abstruse or doubtful problems.

With the same thoughtfulness for the student's progress, the appended Notes provide considerable information outright; but they are also designed to stimulate the student in making researches for himself, as well as in applying, under the direction of the teacher, the principles laid down in the critical examination of the separate divisions.

A portrait, either of the author or of the personage about whom he writes, will form an attractive feature of each volume. The text is from approved editions, keeping as far as possible the original form; and the contents offer, at a very reasonable price, the latest results of critical instruction in the art of literary expression.

The teacher will appreciate the fact that enough, and not too much, assistance is rendered the student, leaving the instructor ample room for applying and extending the principles and suggestions which have been presented.

INTRODUCTION.

Thomas De Quincey is among the unique personalities in modern English literature. With a countenance remarkable for its intellectual quality and every appearance of high breeding, his smallness of stature was soon forgotten when his conversational powers, in which he excelled, exercised their fascination over the listener.

In like manner, one forgets, while reading his voluminous writings, that he was an opium eater for many years of his life; and, were it not for his autobiographic sketches, including "The Confessions of an English Opium Eater" and "Suspiria," there would be little suspicion that his life was "shadowed by one great cloud, which would have fatally obscured any ordinary intellect."

The materials for a description of his early years, and of his struggle with and final victory over the "narcotic devil," are drawn from his own writings, mainly from those which have been mentioned.

Ample data, however, of his literary habits are given in the reminiscences of his friends, who regarded him as a great literary genius.

We will consider the incidents of his career chiefly as they bear a relation to his works, in which scholarship, imagination, wit, and humor combine to make him one of the most attractive, as well as instructive, writers of his period.

That period is justly celebrated for its constellation of famous authors, often styled the Lake Poets of England, living as they did among the beautiful scenery of the Westmoreland lakes.

The father of De Quincey was a merchant, who died when his son was seven years old, leaving a comfortable inheritance to his children. Thomas was placed, by his father's will, under the care of four guardians, who sent him successively to several schools. At thirteen years of age he wrote Greek with ease; at fifteen, he could converse fluently in that language, and when at Eton he was the phenomenal scholar of his class.

Being ready for the university in his sixteenth year, he requested his guardian, under whose sole care he had then come, to allow him to leave Eton. The guardian, a worthy but obstinate man, refused; this disturbed the lad and touched his pride, so that on his seventeenth birthday he ran away, wandered through North Wales, and eventually reached London, without money but determined to elude all pursuit.

Now began a long agony of extremity and hunger, which lasted many months. Finally, he applied to a Jew, and, on the strength of his financial expectations, raised the money to carry him in pursuit of a classmate, who he hoped would aid him in his wish for a course at the university.

His errand was fruitless; but soon a reconciliation,

effected partly by accident, was made with his friends, and his uncle sent him to Worcester College, Oxford, with an allowance of £100 a year.

Unfortunately his abject, though voluntary, penury in London had so affected his constitution that he soon fell under the fearful habit of eating opium.

In the first part of his "Confessions," entitled, "The Pleasures of Opium," he tells us that he experienced only enjoyable sensations from 1804 until 1812. After the latter year, his chapter on "The Pains of Opium" describes the miseries into which the fearful habit plunged him, body and mind. These "Confessions" were first published in 1821, but were given to the world in their final form in 1856.

It is not necessary to trace the series of struggles, relapses, and comparative escape at last, which checkered his life with reveries, moods, brilliant episodes, and periods of incapacity. So far as his literary career was affected by his use of opium, it must be said, that, while the best of his works are the result of his genius and industry, undoubtedly much of his impassioned prose, his dreamy and fantastic descriptions, his sense of the vast and the vague, may be attributed to the effect upon his brain of the pernicious drug.

It is a marvel that, notwithstanding the phantoms, incommunicable in words, which haunted his mind, he preserved to the last a fine literary instinct and a sweetness and courtesy of manner which lend a charm to almost everything he wrote.

Even in his autobiographical writings, he maintained a

self-respect, which is evident in the purity of his imagery and in the high moral tone of his sentiments. There was a certain reticence which respected his own private rights as a man, and which calls for the reader's extenuation rather than hasty condemnation of his fault. His choice of subjects was sometimes on the unprofitable side, as in his ingenious defense of Judas Iscariot, his "Murder as a Fine Art," and in "The Vision of Sudden Death." His discursive style, in much of his writing, seems involved and incomplete, and his idealizing tendency often leads to exaggeration; but, take him all in all, De Quincey well merits what Christopher North said of him in "Noctes Ambrosianæ," that "with all his logic, he is a man of imagination; and, bating a little formal pedantry now and then, a master of the English language; God bless him!"

Archdeacon Hare calls him "the great logician of our times." Coleridge, addicted to the same opium habit, thought much of his literary ability. Both Coleridge and De Quincey were equally gifted in the flow and the breadth of their conversation; but the great author of "Aids to Reflection" was much more averse to the labors of composition than De Quincey.

Both were scholars at Eton, although Coleridge was thirteen years older than his friend, having been born in 1772, and De Quincey in 1785 (at Greenheys, near Manchester). They were graduated from different universities, Coleridge being a Cambridge and De Quincey an Oxford man. They did not meet until 1807; but when De Quincey settled at Grasmere, in 1809 (holding a cottage there for twenty-seven years), he was at once admitted into the charmed circle of his literary neighbors, among whom Coleridge, Wordsworth, Southey, and Charles Lloyd were preëminent.

Charles Lamb, who had befriended him in his early days, was also one of the choice spirits whom he termed "princely" both in generosity and friendship.

De Quincey was married in 1816. He had five sons and three daughters. After his removal to Scotland, he edited, in 1819, *The Westmoreland Gazette*, but in 1821, a large part of his patrimony having wasted away, he went to London and remained till 1824, writing and publishing his "Confessions," and contributing to *The London Magazine*.

After vibrating between London and Grasmere, we find him in 1828 at Edinburgh, where he wrote for *Blackwood's Magazine* and other reviews, and where he joined the famous coterie, consisting of John Wilson (Christopher North), Hogg (the Ettrick Shepherd), and others, whose wise (and foolish) "convivia" are chronicled in the celebrated "Noctes Ambrosianæ."

For convenience, he had his family with him in Edinburgh several years, still keeping the Grasmere cottage. His wife died in 1837, when his eldest daughter became the able mistress of the household. In 1840 he accompanied his daughters to Lasswade, which was his home for the rest of his life, although he spent about three years in astronomical researches in Glasgow and was often in Edinburgh. He died at Edinburgh in the seventy-fifth year of his age, December 8, 1859.

The range of De Quincey's literary works is very wide;

historical, biographical, theological, and miscellaneous, not to speak of his fanciful and mystic lucubrations, all of which form a notable part of the English literature of the early half of the nineteenth century. His eccentricities were as marked as his genius. He gave away money lavishly, and polished his shillings before he handed them to the beggars. He left bushels of papers in lodging houses, and forgot where he had deposited them. He was often "snowed in" by heaps of useless journals and manuscripts in his rooms, and was Bohemian in his impulses and manners.

But when his antiquated figure, quaintly dressed, was seen no more in the streets of old Edinburgh, the critics might complain of his discursive tendency and infinite subtlety, but no one could deny that he possessed the musical element in style, a mystic beauty of imagery, a conscience in literary effort, and a charm in simple narration, which few writers of the English language have equaled and none have excelled.

That his heart was gentle is proved by his attachment to children and his generosity to the poor; that, in the midst of his failings and eccentricities, his sensibilities were elevated and pure, is gathered from his acts and words, as when he said of the animals and birds which he loved, "The instincts of all the inferior creatures are now holy in my eyes; for, like reason's self, they have their origin in love." And so we leave him gently and kindly, with his biographer's remark, "*Nil tangit quod non ornat.*"

THE ART OF NARRATION

AS ILLUSTRATED IN

DE QUINCEY'S "FLIGHT OF A TARTAR TRIBE."

In prose literature, the art of narration is distinct by itself. It may be joined with other forms of composition, in historical and biographical writing, and in the essay; but there are rules which regulate it that cannot be overlooked.

Few possess the gift of story-telling in perfection. The art may be acquired by study and practice; only the rare literary genius can possess it without laborious effort.

Narration, pure and simple, is not historical composition, although it may give historical events. The historian employs generalization and argument, and sums up the conclusions of authorities. He ought not to argue as a partisan. De Quincey censures the historian Hume for doing this. Neither should he encumber his work with gossipy tales, becoming, as De Quincey styles Suetonius, author of the Lives of the Twelve Cæsars, "a curious collector of anecdotage." But the historian, as such, may use reasoning and logic, of which the narrator has little need.

The writer of narrative must have events to tell, and be able to tell them in a way that will hold the reader's interest to the end. He will arrange his materials in a natural sequence, and have the whole story in his mind as he writes, so as to avoid repetition and a premature disclosure of the ending of his story.

But rhetorical writing, elocution, argument, and dissertation are foreign to his purpose. Long-winded disquisitions and digressions are out of place in narration. There is a vast difference between a classic flow of language and the spinning of long yarns.

The narrator's vocabulary need not be very large, but he will have full command of appropriate words. De Quincey said that in early life he labored under a "peculiar penury of words." Later on, he acquired sufficient command of language, and was sometimes perplexed by an exuberance of expressive terms.

Long sentences may be allowed in narration, if the language is clear and the connectives are well chosen. But parenthetical clauses ought generally to be avoided as inelegant in literary style, and especially in this department of composition. "A parenthesis is a chasm," says a critic of style, "across which it is hard for the reader to leap."

Classical allusions are permitted in narration when they reinforce the writer's descriptions, or help to explain his story; never should they be used for mere embellishment. An acquaintance with the best Latin and Greek authors is, however, of advantage, inasmuch as writers like Herodotus, Homer in some parts of the "Iliad," and Cæsar in his "Commentaries," are models of this form of composition.

De Quincey was familiar from his youth with the ancient

classics, and their influence on him gave precision and elegance to his style. But he uses some words of foreign derivation where Saxon would have been more to the point. Coleridge sacrificed much to his German models, and thereby led his readers into many a mystic maze.

Clearness and simplicity are indispensable to good narration. What Sydney Smith calls "obvious language" is essential, because no narrative can be perfect which compels the reader to read a sentence twice before he can get at the meaning of it. Herbert Spencer advises literary men to "economize the mental force of their readers"; and in no department of literature is this advice more to be heeded than in the telling of a story.

Simplicity in the manner of describing men and events makes narration a delight. Long descriptions of scenery, which do not add to the understanding of the plot, are generally skipped by the reader, who is promised a story and who does not want to be delayed by fine writing in the progress of the tale. An unaffected style is always graceful and acceptable, especially when the writer professes to be a narrator of facts.

Now, De Quincey may not be the writer who will give the best model in all respects for a perfect English style; he writes in various moods, and sometimes wanders away into strange vagaries of expression. But he certainly offers a very fair example of narration in his story of The Revolt of the Tartars and their tragic flight. Here, at least, there is no "soaring in a winged chariot on a figurative vocabulary." He has declared that, "through a circle of prodigious reading, he had never known a writer who did not sometimes violate the accidence or syntax of the English language," so that we cannot expect him to be the sole exception to this general affirmation. In the paper, however, which we are about to study, the art of narration is brought very near perfection.

The story flows easily along. It is not broken up by irrelevant dissertations on things that are foreign to it. As you read, with sustained interest to the end, you do not think of the writer, who also seems to have forgotten himself in his work, and you mind what he is telling rather than how he is telling it.

He may have erred in the first few prefatory pages, which naturally belong at the end of the story because they contain remarks about things which the reader can understand only as he follows the narrative itself.

But, beginning with the story proper at the sentence "On the 21st of January, 1761" (p. 21), we find few if any violations of the canons laid down for this kind of literary work.

There are some long paragraphs. Take, for example, the description (p. 22) of the young Kalmuck prince, Oubacha; but notice how skillfully the author uses the connectives of the clauses, giving the reader no trouble with the length of the whole sentence.

The writer introduces to the reader early in the narrative all that needs to be said about the character of the treacherous pretender, Zebek-Dorchi. This is art, for it obviates the necessity for any further statement, in this respect, as the story progresses.

Almost the only place in which the narrator volunteers

an opinion of his own is (p. 26) in the few paragraphs beginning, "He, a worm as he was," etc.,—an allowable analysis of the traitor's mental attitude, because, without this explanation, the traitor's cause would seem utterly reckless and foolhardy.

Now and then, as in the sentence (p. 31) "Human experience gives evidence," etc., the author departs from pure narration and states a general proposition. In this case, as the proposition is by no means a truism, it should not have been interpolated, because it needs proofs which this is not the place to give.

The slight digression (p. 31) on the war between Russia and the Sultan is allowable, because it explains why Oubacha contributed more than his quota of cavalry on the eve of the intended flight, and because it is necessary to show the favorable and unfavorable results of his splendid victories over the Turks. These results were unfavorable to the scheme in hand, because the jealousy and hostility of certain tribes were aroused against the migrating Kalmucks; and they were favorable to the scheme, by preparing the minds of the Kalmucks themselves to perceive the necessity of instant departure.

Take note, now, how the narrator, after depicting Zebek's shrewd arraignment of Russia's tyranny before the assembled representatives of the Kalmuck tribes (pp. 38–41), hurries on the story, till on the 5th of January, 1762 (see p. 41), the multitudes begin their migration.

From this point onward, the reader is led from one scene of horror to another, through the awful series of calamities; worse, as the writer declares, than the inroads of Huns, Avars, or Mongol Tartars brought upon their victims; worse than the sufferings of Napoleon's army in the retreat from Moscow, which the writer delays but a moment to consider.

It is a lengthy narrative; yet it cannot be shortened, in justice to the subject and the reader's demand for details. A single allusion to Xerxes (p. 56) is all that this lover of classic legend allows himself to make.

The episode (p. 60) which describes the rescue of Oubacha, the Khan, from the treachery of his unprincipled cousin, Zebek, is a thrilling incident, which heightens the description of this agonizing flight of the wretched Kalmucks.

It is at this point, by a stroke of genius, that the narrator relieves the reader's mind from its terrible strain by bringing on the scene, before the final catastrophe at the Lake of Tengis, Kien Long, the Emperor of China, whose munificence relieved the necessities of the survivors of the flight, and gave them territorial possessions under his protection.

Without this relief for a moment, the overwhelming horrors of the carnage at the bloody lake would be insupportable to the reader, leaving him in a tumult of indescribable emotions.

Finally, when Zebek-Dorchi, the arch-traitor, is disposed of by assassination, at an imperial banquet, even poetic justice is satisfied, and the story-teller leaves the decimated Tartar tribe in the midst of quiet sylvan scenes, rich in all the luxuries of life and the loveliness of Arcadian beauty, where their descendants remain unto this day.

In all this De Quincey has shown the art of a true narrator. The story which he tells is derived from veritable history. But his genius appears, in that, while the narrative does not deviate from historic fact, nor dress the characters in artificial garb, nor color the incidents with adventitious horrors, the reader is borne on to the end with ever-increasing interest, absorbed in the story without thinking of the style.

It is plain, concise, classic, dealing with events as they occurred, and with men as they actually lived, fought, and suffered. The hand of a master has thus prepared in literature, to the memory of the princely Oubacha and his afflicted countrymen, a monument more enduring than the mighty columns of granite and brass erected near the banks of the Ily, by the Chinese Emperor, to commemorate with appropriate inscriptions,

THE FLIGHT OF A TARTAR TRIBE.

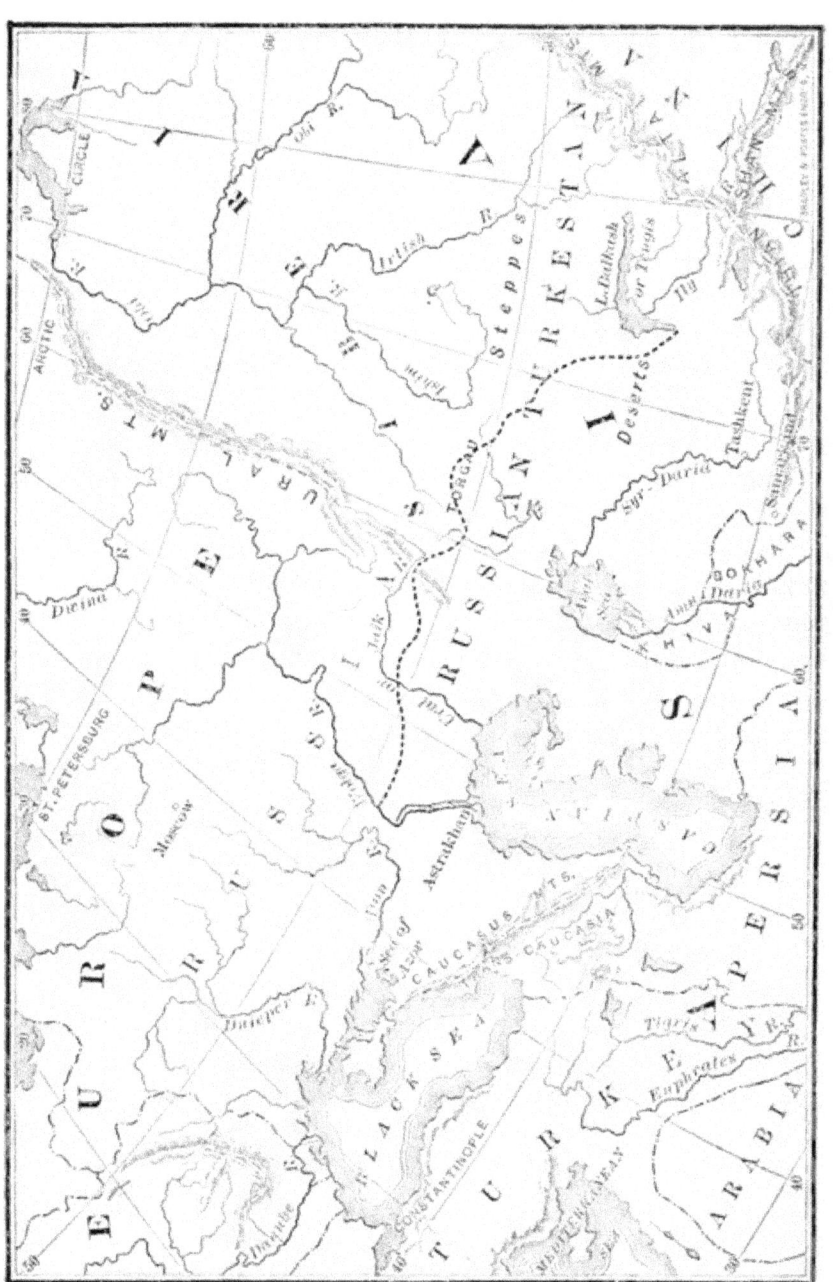

PART OF CENTRAL ASIA.

The Dotted Line shows the Supposed Route of the Flight of the Tartar Tribe. A.D. 1771.

DE QUINCEY'S
FLIGHT OF A TARTAR TRIBE.

THERE is no great event in modern history, or, perhaps it may be said more broadly, none in all history from its earliest records, less generally known, or more striking to the imagination, than the flight eastwards of a principal Tartar nation across the boundless steppes of Asia in the latter half of the last century. The *terminus a quo* of this flight and the *terminus ad quem* are equally magnificent, — the mightiest of Christian thrones being the one, the mightiest of Pagan the other. And the grandeur of these two terminal objects is harmoniously supported by the romantic circumstances of the flight. In the abruptness of its commencement and the fierce velocity of its execution, we read an expression of the wild, barbaric character of those who conducted the movement. In the unity of purpose connecting this myriad of wills, and in the blind but unerring aim at a mark so remote, there is something which recalls to the mind those almighty instincts that propel the migrations of the swallow and the lemming, or the life-withering marches of the locust. Then, again, in the gloomy vengeance of Russia and her vast artillery, which hung upon the rear and the skirts of the fugitive vassals, we are reminded of Miltonic images, — such, for instance, as that of the solitary hand pursuing through desert spaces and through ancient chaos a rebellious host, and overtaking with volleying thunders those who believed themselves already within the security of darkness and of distance.

We shall have occasion, further on, to compare this event with other great national catastrophes as to the magnitude of the suffering; but it may also challenge a comparison with similar events under another relation, viz., as to its dramatic capabilities. Few cases, perhaps, in romance or history, can sustain a close collation with this as to the complexity of its separate interests. The great outline of the enterprise, taken in connection with the operative motives, hidden or avowed, and the religious sanctions under which it was pursued, give to the case a triple character: First, That of a *conspiracy*, with as close a unity in the incidents, and as much of a personal interest in the moving characters, with fine dramatic contrasts, as belongs to *Venice Preserved* or to the *Fiesco* of Schiller. Secondly, That of a great *military expedition*, offering the same romantic features of vast distances to be traversed, vast reverses to be sustained, untried routes, enemies obscurely ascertained, and hardships too vaguely prefigured, which mark the Egyptian expedition of Cambyses; the anabasis of the younger Cyrus, and the subsequent retreat of the ten thousand to the Black Sea; the Parthian expeditions of the Romans, especially those of Crassus and Julian; or (as more disastrous than any of them, and, in point of space as well as in amount of forces, more extensive) the Russian anabasis and katabasis of Napoleon. Thirdly, That of a *religious exodus*, authorized by an oracle venerated throughout many nations of Asia, — an exodus, therefore, in so far resembling the great scriptural exodus of the Israelites under Moses and Joshua, as well as in the very peculiar distinction of carrying along with them their entire families, women, children, slaves, their herds of cattle and of sheep, their horses and their camels.

This triple character of the enterprise naturally invests it

with a more comprehensive interest. But the dramatic
interest which we ascribed to it, or its fitness for a stage
representation, depends partly upon the marked variety
and the strength of the personal agencies concerned, and
partly upon the succession of scenical situations. Even
the steppes, the camels, the tents, the snowy and the sandy
deserts, are not beyond the scale of our modern representative powers as often called into action in the theatres both
of Paris and London; and the series of situations unfolded,
beginning with the general conflagration on the Wolga, pass-
ing thence to the disastrous scenes of the flight (as it liter-
ally was in its commencement), to the Tartar siege of the
Russian fortress Koulagina; the bloody engagement with
the Cossacks in the mountain passes at Ouchim; the sur-
prisal by the Bashkirs and the advanced posts of the Russian army at Torgau; the private conspiracy at this point
against the khan; the long succession of running fights;
the parting massacres at the Lake of Tengis under the eyes
of the Chinese; and, finally, the tragical retribution to
Zebek-Dorchi at the hunting lodge of the Chinese Emperor,
— all these situations communicate a scenical animation to
the wild romance, if treated dramatically; whilst a higher
and a philosophic interest belongs to it as a case of authen-
tic history, commemorating a great revolution for good and
for evil in the fortunes of a whole people, — a people semi-
barbarous, but simple-hearted and of ancient descent.

On the 21st of January, 1761, the young Prince Oubacha
assumed the sceptre of the Kalmucks upon the death of his
father. Some part of the power attached to this dignity he
had already wielded since his fourteenth year, in quality of
vice-khan, by the express appointment and with the avowed
support of the Russian government. He was now about
eighteen years of age, amiable in his personal character,
and not without titles to respect in his public character as

a sovereign prince. In times more peaceable, and amongst a people more entirely civilized or more humanized by religion, it is even probable that he might have discharged his high duties with considerable distinction. But his lot was thrown upon stormy times, and a most difficult crisis amongst tribes whose native ferocity was exasperated by debasing forms of superstition, and by a nationality as well as an inflated conceit of their own merit absolutely unparalleled; whilst the circumstances of their hard and trying position under the jealous surveillance of an irresistible lord paramount, in the person of the Russian Czar, gave a fiercer edge to the natural unamiableness of the Kalmuck disposition, and irritated its gloomier qualities into action under the restless impulses of suspicion and permanent distrust. No prince could hope for a cordial allegiance from his subjects or a peaceful reign under the circumstances of the case; for the dilemma in which a Kalmuck ruler stood at present was of this nature: *wanting* the sanction and support of the Czar, he was inevitably too weak from without to command confidence from his subjects, or resistance to his competitors: on the other hand, *with* this kind of support, and deriving his title in any degree from the favor of the imperial court, he became almost in that extent an object of hatred at home and within the whole compass of his own territory. He was at once an object of hatred for the past, being a living monument of national independence ignominiously surrendered, and an object of jealousy for the future, as one who had already advertised himself to be a fitting tool for the ultimate purposes (whatsoever those might prove to be) of the Russian court. Coming himself to the Kalmuck sceptre under the heaviest weight of prejudice from the unfortunate circumstances of his position, it might have been expected that Oubacha would have been pre-eminently an object of detestation; for, besides his known dependence upon the cabinet of St.

Petersburg, the direct line of succession had been set aside, and the principle of inheritance violently suspended, in favor of his own father, so recently as nineteen years before the era of his own accession, consequently within the lively remembrance of the existing generation. He therefore, almost equally with his father, stood within the full current of the national prejudices, and might have anticipated the most pointed hostility. But it was not so: such are the caprices in human affairs that he was even, in a moderate sense, popular,— a benefit which wore the more cheering aspect and the promises of permanence, inasmuch as he owed it exclusively to his personal qualities of kindness and affability, as well as to the beneficence of his government. On the other hand, to balance this unlooked-for prosperity at the outset of his reign, he met with a rival in popular favor, almost a competitor, in the person of Zebek-Dorchi, a prince with considerable pretensions to the throne, and perhaps, it might be said, with equal pretensions. Zebek-Dorchi was a direct descendant of the same royal house as himself, through a different branch. On public grounds his claim stood, perhaps, on a footing equally good with that of Oubacha; whilst his personal qualities, even in those aspects which seemed to a philosophical observer most odious and repulsive, promised the most effectual aid to the dark purposes of an intriguer or a conspirator, and were generally fitted to win a popular support precisely in those points where Oubacha was most defective. He was much superior in external appearance to his rival on the throne, and so far better qualified to win the good opinion of a semi-barbarous people; whilst his dark intellectual qualities of Machiavelian dissimulation, profound hypocrisy, and perfidy which knew no touch of remorse, were admirably calculated to sustain any ground which he might win from the simple-hearted people with whom he had to deal, and from the frank carelessness of his unconscious competitor.

At the very outset of his treacherous career, Zebek-Dorchi was sagacious enough to perceive that nothing could be gained by open declaration of hostility to the reigning prince: the choice had been a deliberate act on the part of Russia, and Elizabeth Petrowna was not the person to recall her own favors with levity or upon slight grounds. Openly, therefore, to have declared his enmity towards his relative on the throne could have had no effect but that of arming suspicions against his own ulterior purposes in a quarter where it was most essential to his interest that for the present all suspicion should be hoodwinked. Accordingly, after much meditation, the course he took for opening his snares was this: He raised a rumor that his own life was in danger from the plots of several *saissang* (that is, Kalmuck nobles) who were leagued together under an oath to assassinate him; and immediately after, assuming a well-counterfeited alarm, he fled to Tcherkask, followed by sixty-five tents. From this place he kept up a correspondence with the imperial court, and, by way of soliciting his cause more effectually, he soon repaired in person to St. Petersburg. Once admitted to personal conferences with the cabinet, he found no difficulty in winning over the Russian councils to a concurrence with some of his political views, and thus covertly introducing the point of that wedge which was finally to accomplish his purposes. In particular, he persuaded the Russian government to make a very important alteration in the constitution of the Kalmuck state council, which in effect reorganized the whole political condition of the state and disturbed the balance of power as previously adjusted. Of this council, in the Kalmuck language called *sarga*, there were eight members, called *sargatchi;* and hitherto it had been the custom that these eight members should be entirely subordinate to the khan, holding, in fact, the ministerial character of secretaries and assistants, but in no respect ranking as co-ordinate authorities. That had produced some inconveniences in former reigns; and it was easy for Zebek-Dorchi to point the jealousy of the Russian court to others more serious which might arise in future circumstances of war or other contingencies. It was resolved, therefore, to place the *sargatchi* henceforward on a footing of perfect independence, and therefore (as regarded responsibility) on a footing of equality with the khan. Their independence, however, had respect only to their own sovereign; for towards Russia they were placed in a new attitude of direct duty and accountability by the creation in their favor of small pensions (three hundred roubles a year), which, however, to a Kalmuck of that day, were more considerable than might be supposed, and had a further value as marks of honorary distinction emanating from a great empress. Thus far the purposes of Zebek-Dorchi were served effectually for the moment; but apparently it was only for the moment, since, in the further development of his plots, this very dependency upon Russian influence would be the most serious obstacle in his way. There was, however, another point carried, which outweighed all inferior considerations, as it gave him a power of setting aside discretionally whatsoever should arise to disturb his plots: he was himself appointed president and controller of the *sargatchi*. The Russian court had been aware of his high pretensions by birth, and hoped by this promotion to satisfy the ambition which, in some degree, was acknowledged to be a reasonable passion for any man occupying his situation.

Having thus completely blindfolded the cabinet of Russia, Zebek-Dorchi proceeded in his new character to fulfil his political mission with the khan of the Kalmucks. So artfully did he prepare the road for his favorable reception at the court of this prince, that he was at once and universally welcomed as a public benefactor. The pensions of the councillors were so much additional wealth poured into the

Tartar exchequer: as to the ties of dependency thus created, experience had not yet enlightened these simple tribes as to that result. And that he himself should be the chief of these mercenary councillors was so far from being charged upon Zebek as any offence, or any ground of suspicion, that his relative the khan returned him hearty thanks for his services, under the belief that he could have accepted this appointment only with a view to keep out other and more unwelcome pretenders, who would not have had the same motives of consanguinity or friendship for executing its duties in a spirit of kindness to the Kalmucks. The first use which he made of his new functions about the khan's person was to attack the court of Russia, by a romantic villainy not easy to be credited, for those very acts of interference with the council which he himself had prompted. This was a dangerous step; but it was indispensable to his farther advance upon the gloomy path which he had traced out for himself. A triple vengeance was what he meditated: (1) upon the Russian cabinet, for having undervalued his own pretensions to the throne; (2) upon his amiable rival, for having supplanted him; and (3) upon all those of the nobility who had manifested their sense of his weakness by their neglect, or their sense of his perfidious character by their suspicions. Here was a colossal outline of wickedness; and by one in his situation, feeble (as it might seem) for the accomplishment of its humblest parts, how was the total edifice to be reared in its comprehensive grandeur? He, a worm as he was, could he venture to assail the mighty behemoth of Muscovy, the potentate who counted three hundred languages around the footsteps of his throne, and from whose "lion ramp" recoiled alike "baptized and infidel," — Christendom on the one side, strong by her intellect and her organization, and the "barbaric East" on the other, with her unnumbered numbers? The match was a monstrous one;

but in its very monstrosity there lay this germ of encouragement, — that it could not be suspected. The very hopelessness of the scheme grounded his hope; and he resolved to execute a vengeance which should involve, as it were, in the unity of a well-laid tragic fable, all whom he judged to be his enemies. That vengeance lay in detaching from the Russian Empire the whole Kalmuck nation, and breaking up that system of intercourse which had thus far been beneficial to both. This last was a consideration which moved him but little. True it was that Russia to the Kalmucks had secured lands and extensive pasturage; true it was that the Kalmucks reciprocally to Russia had furnished a powerful cavalry. But the latter loss would be part of his triumph, and the former might be more than compensated in other climates, under other sovereigns. Here was a scheme, which, in its final accomplishment, would avenge him bitterly on the Czarina, and in the course of its accomplishment might furnish him with ample occasions for removing his other enemies. It may be readily supposed, indeed, that he who could deliberately raise his eyes to the Russian autocrat as an antagonist in single duel with himself was not likely to feel much anxiety about Kalmuck enemies of whatever rank. He took his resolution, therefore, sternly and irrevocably to effect this astonishing translation of an ancient people across the pathless deserts of Central Asia, intersected continually by rapid rivers rarely furnished with bridges, and of which the fords were known only to those who might think it for their interest to conceal them, through many nations inhospitable or hostile, — frost and snow around them (from the necessity of commencing their flight in the winter), famine in their front, and the sabre, or even the artillery, of an offended and mighty empress hanging upon their rear for thousands of miles. But what was to be their final mark, the port of shelter after so fearful a course of wandering? Two things were evident: it must be some power at a great distance from Russia, so as to make return even in that view hopeless; and it must be a power of sufficient rank to insure them protection from any hostile efforts on the part of the Czarina for reclaiming them or for chastising their revolt. Both conditions were united obviously in the person of Kien Long, the reigning Emperor of China, who was further recommended to them by his respect for the head of their religion. To China, therefore, and, as their first rendezvous, to the shadow of the great Chinese Wall, it was settled by Zebek that they should direct their flight.

Next came the question of time: *When* should the flight commence? and, finally, the more delicate question as to the choice of accomplices. To extend the knowledge of the conspiracy too far was to insure its betrayal to the Russian government. Yet, at some stage of the preparations it was evident that a very extensive confidence must be made, because in no other way could the mass of the Kalmuck population be persuaded to furnish their families with the requisite equipments for so long a migration. This critical step, however, it was resolved to defer up to the latest possible moment, and at all events to make no general communication on the subject until the time of departure should be definitely settled. In the meantime Zebek admitted only three persons to his confidence, of whom Oubacha, the reigning prince, was almost necessarily one; but him, from his yielding and somewhat feeble character, he viewed rather in the light of a tool than as one of his active accomplices. Those whom (if anybody) he admitted to an unreserved participation in his counsels were two only,— the great lama among the Kalmucks, and his own father-in-law, Erempel, a ruling prince of some tribe in the neighborhood of the Caspian Sea, recommended to his favor not so much by any strength of talent corresponding to the occasion, as by his blind devotion to him-

self and his passionate anxiety to promote the elevation of
his daughter and his son-in-law to the throne of a sovereign
prince. A titular prince, Zebek already was; but this dignity, without the substantial accompaniment of a sceptre,
seemed but an empty sound to both of these ambitious
rivals. The other accomplice, whose name was Loosang-
Dchaltzan, and whose rank was that of lama, or Kalmuck
pontiff, was a person of far more distinguished pretensions.
He had something of the same gloomy and terrific pride
which marked the character of Zebek himself, manifesting
also the same energy, accompanied by the same unfaltering
cruelty, and a natural facility of dissimulation even more
profound. It was by this man that the other question was
settled as to the time for giving effect to their designs.
His own pontifical character had suggested to him, that in
order to strengthen their influence with the vast mob of
simple-minded men whom they were to lead into a howling
wilderness, after persuading them to lay desolate their own
ancient hearths, it was indispensable that they should be
able, in cases of extremity, to plead the express sanction of
God for their entire enterprise. This could only be done
by addressing themselves to the great head of their religion,— the dalai-lama of Thibet. Him they easily per
suaded to countenance their schemes; and an oracle was
delivered solemnly at Thibet, to the effect that no ultimate
prosperity would attend this great exodus unless it were
pursued through the years of the *tiger* and the *hare*. Now,
the Kalmuck custom is to distinguish their years by attach-
ing to each a denomination taken from one of twelve animals, the exact order of succession being absolutely fixed;
so that the cycle revolves, of course, through a period of a
dozen years. Consequently, if the approaching year of the
tiger were suffered to escape them, in that case the expedition must be delayed for twelve years more; within which
period, even were no other unfavorable changes to arise, it

was pretty well foreseen that the Russian government would
take the most effectual means for bridling their vagrant
propensities by a ring fence of forts, or military posts, to
say nothing of the still readier plan for securing their fidel-
ity (a plan already talked of in all quarters) by exacting
a large body of hostages selected from the families of the
most influential nobles. On these cogent considerations it
was solemnly determined that this terrific experiment should
be made in the next year of the *tiger*, which happened to
fall upon the Christian year 1771. With respect to the
month, there was, unhappily for the Kalmucks, even less
latitude allowed to their choice than with respect to the
year. It was absolutely necessary, or it was thought so,
that the different divisions of the nation, which pastured
their flocks on both banks of the Wolga, should have the
means of effecting an instantaneous junction, because the
danger of being intercepted by flying columns of the imperial armies was precisely the greatest at the outset. Now,
from the want of bridges, or sufficient river craft for trans-
porting so vast a body of men, the sole means which could
be depended upon (especially where so many women, children, and camels were concerned) was *ice;* and this, in a
state of sufficient firmness, could not be absolutely counted
upon before the month of January. Hence it happened
that this astonishing exodus of a whole nation — before so
much as a whisper of the design had begun to circulate
amongst those whom it most interested, before it was even
suspected that any man's wishes pointed in that direction —
had been definitively appointed for January of the year 1771;
and, almost up to the Christmas of 1770, the poor, simple
Kalmuck herdsmen and their families were going nightly to
their peaceful beds without even dreaming that the fiat had
already gone forth from their rulers, consigning those quiet
abodes, together with the peace and comfort which reigned
within them, to a withering desolation, now close at hand.

Meantime war raged on a great scale between Russia and the Sultan; and, until the time arrived for throwing off their vassalage, it was necessary that Oubacha should contribute his usual contingent of martial aid. Nay, it had unfortunately become prudent that he should contribute a much more than his usual aid. Human experience gives ample evidence that in some mysterious and unaccountable way no great design is ever agitated, no matter how few or how faithful may be the participators, but that some presentiment, some dim misgiving, is kindled amongst those whom it is chiefly important to blind. And, however it might have happened, certain it is that already, when as yet no syllable of the conspiracy had been breathed to any man whose very existence was not staked upon its concealment, nevertheless some vague and uneasy jealousy had arisen in the Russian cabinet as to the future schemes of the Kalmuck khan; and very probable it is, that, but for the war then raging and the consequent prudence of conciliating a very important vassal, or at least of abstaining from what would powerfully alienate him, even at that moment such measures would have been adopted as must forever have intercepted the Kalmuck schemes. Slight as were the jealousies of the imperial court, they had not escaped the Machiavellian eyes of Zebek and the lama; and under their guidance, Oubacha, bending to the circumstances of the moment, and meeting the jealousy of the Russian court with a policy corresponding to their own, strove by unusual zeal to efface the Czarina's unfavorable impressions. He enlarged the scale of his contributions, and that so prodigiously, that he absolutely carried to headquarters a force of thirty-five thousand cavalry, fully equipped. Some go further, and rate the amount beyond forty thousand; but the smaller estimate is, at all events, within the truth.

With this magnificent array of cavalry, heavy as well as

light, the khan went into the field under great expectations; and these he more than realized. Having the good fortune to be concerned with so ill-organized and disorderly a description of force as that which at all times composed the bulk of a Turkish army, he carried victory along with his banners, gained many partial successes, and at last, in a pitched battle, overthrew the Turkish force opposed to him, with a loss of five thousand men left upon the field.

These splendid achievements seemed likely to operate in various ways against the impending revolt. Oubacha had now a strong motive, in the martial glory acquired, for continuing his connection with the empire in whose service he had won it, and by whom only it could be fully appreciated. He was now a great marshal of a great empire, — one of the paladins around the imperial throne; in China he would be nobody, or (worse than that) a mendicant alien, prostrate at the feet, and soliciting the precarious alms, of a prince with whom he had no connection. Besides, it might reasonably be expected that the Czarina, grateful for the really efficient aid given by the Tartar prince, would confer upon him such eminent rewards as might be sufficient to anchor his hopes upon Russia and to wean him from every possible seduction. These were the obvious suggestions of prudence and good sense to every man who stood neutral in the case. But they were disappointed. The Czarina knew her obligations to the khan; but she did not acknowledge them. Wherefore? That is a mystery perhaps never to be explained. So it was, however. The khan went unhonored; no ukase ever proclaimed his merits; and perhaps, had he even been abundantly recompensed by Russia, there were others who would have defeated these tendencies to reconciliation. Erempel, Zebek, and Loosang, the lama, were pledged life-deep to prevent any accommodation; and their efforts were unfortunately seconded by those of their deadliest enemies. In the Russian court there were at that time some great nobles preoccupied with feelings of hatred and blind malice towards the Kalmucks, quite as strong as any which the Kalmucks could harbor towards Russia, and not, perhaps, so well founded. Just as much as the Kalmucks hated the Russian yoke, their galling assumption of authority, the marked air of disdain, as towards a nation of ugly, stupid, and filthy barbarians, which too generally marked the Russian bearing and language,— but, above all, the insolent contempt, or even outrages, which the Russian governors or great military commandants tolerated in their followers towards the barbarous religion and superstitious mummeries of the Kalmuck priesthood,— precisely in that extent did the ferocity of the Russian resentment, and their wrath at seeing the trampled worm turn, or attempt a feeble retaliation, react upon the unfortunate Kalmucks. At this crisis it is probable that envy and wounded pride, upon witnessing the splendid victories of Oubacha and Momotbacha over the Turks and Bashkirs, contributed strength to the Russian irritation; and it must have been through the intrigues of those nobles about her person who chiefly smarted under these feelings, that the Czarina could ever have lent herself to the unwise and ungrateful policy pursued at this critical period towards the Kalmuck khan. That Czarina was no longer Elizabeth Petrowna: it was Catharine II., a princess who did not often err so injuriously (injuriously for herself as much as for others) in the measures of her government. She had soon ample reason for repenting of her false policy. Meantime, how much it must have co-operated with the other motives previously acting upon Oubacha in sustaining his determination to revolt, and how powerfully it must have assisted the efforts of all the Tartar chieftains in preparing the minds of their people to feel the necessity of this difficult enterprise, by arming their pride and their suspicions against the Russian government, through the keenness of their sympathy with the wrongs of their insulted prince, may be readily imagined. It is a fact, and it has been confessed by candid Russians themselves when treating of this great dismemberment, that the conduct of the Russian cabinet throughout the period of suspense, and during the crisis of hesitation in the Kalmuck council, was exactly such as was most desirable for the purposes of the conspirators: it was such, in fact, as to set the seal to all their machinations, by supplying distinct evidences and official vouchers for what could otherwise have been, at the most, matters of doubtful suspicion and indirect presumption.

Nevertheless, in the face of all these arguments, and even allowing their weight so far as not at all to deny the injustice or the impolicy of the imperial ministers, it is contended by many persons who have reviewed the affair with a command of all the documents bearing on the case, more especially the letters or minutes of council subsequently discovered, in the handwriting of Zebek-Dorchi, and the important evidence of the Russian captive Weseloff, who was carried off by the Kalmucks in their flight, that beyond all doubt Oubacha was powerless for any purpose of impeding or even of delaying the revolt. He himself, indeed, was under religious obligations of the most terrific solemnity never to flinch from the enterprise, or even to slacken in his zeal; for Zebek-Dorchi, distrusting the firmness of his resolution under any unusual pressure of alarm or difficulty, had, in the very earliest stage of the conspiracy, availed himself of the khan's well-known superstition to engage him, by means of previous concert with the priests and their head the lama, in some dark and mysterious rites of consecration, terminating in oaths under such terrific sanctions as no Kalmuck would have courage to violate. As far, therefore, as regarded the personal share of the khan in what was to come, Zebek was entirely at his ease. He

knew him to be so deeply pledged by religious terrors to
the prosecution of the conspiracy that no honors within the
Czarina's gift could have possibly shaken his adhesion; and
then, as to threats from the same quarter, he knew him to
be sealed against those fears by others of a gloomier character, and better adapted to his peculiar temperament. For
Oubacha was a brave man as respected all bodily enemies
or the dangers of human warfare, but was as sensitive and
timid as the most superstitious of old women in facing the
frowns of a priest, or under the vague anticipations of
ghostly retributions. But had it been otherwise, and had
there been any reason to apprehend an unsteady demeanor
on the part of this prince at the approach of the critical
moment, such were the changes already effected in the state
of their domestic politics amongst the Tartars by the undermining arts of Zebek-Dorchi and his ally the lama, that very
little importance would have attached to that doubt. All
power was now effectually lodged in the hand of Zebek-
Dorchi. He was the true and absolute wielder of the Kalmuck sceptre; all measures of importance were submitted
to his discretion, and nothing was finally resolved but under
his dictation. This result he had brought about, in a year
or two, by means sufficiently simple: first of all, by availing
himself of the prejudice in his favor, so largely diffused
among the lowest of the Kalmucks, that his own title to the
throne, in quality of great-grandson in a direct line from
Ajouka, the most illustrious of all the Kalmuck khans,
stood upon a better basis than that of Oubacha, who derived
from a collateral branch; secondly, with respect to that sole
advantage which Oubacha possessed above himself in the
ratification of his title, by improving this difference between
their situations to the disadvantage of his competitor, as
one who had not scrupled to accept that triumph from an
alien power at the price of his independence, which he
himself (as he would have it understood) disdained to court;

thirdly, by his own talents and address, coupled with the
ferocious energy of his moral character; fourthly, and perhaps in an equal degree, by the criminal facility and good
nature of Oubacha; finally (which is remarkable enough, as
illustrating the character of the man), by that very new
modelling of the *sarga*, or privy council, which he had used
as a principal topic of abuse and malicious insinuation
against the Russian government, whilst in reality he first
had suggested the alteration to the empress, and he chiefly
appropriated the political advantages which it was fitted to
yield. For, as he was himself appointed the chief of the
sargatchi, and as the pensions of the inferior *sargatchi* passed
through his hands, whilst in effect they owed their appoint-
ments to his nomination, it may be easily supposed, that
whatever power existed in the state capable of controlling
the khan being held by the *sarga* under its new organization, and this body being completely under his influence,
the final result was to throw all the functions of the state,
whether nominally in the prince or in the council, sub-
stantially into the hands of this one man; whilst at the
same time, from the strict league which he maintained
with the lama, all the thunders of his spiritual power were
always ready to come in aid of the magistrate, or to supply
his incapacity in cases which he could not reach.

But the time was now rapidly approaching for the mighty
experiment. The day was drawing near on which the signal was to be given for raising the standard of revolt, and,
by a combined movement on both sides of the Wolga, for
spreading the smoke of one vast conflagration that should
wrap in a common blaze their own huts and the stately
cities of their enemies over the breadth and length of those
great provinces in which their flocks were dispersed. The
year of the *tiger* was now within one little month of its
commencement. The fifth morning of that year was fixed
for the fatal day when the fortunes and happiness of a

whole nation were to be put upon the hazard of a dicer's throw; and as yet that nation was in profound ignorance of the whole plan. The khan, such was the kindness of his nature, could not bring himself to make the revelation so urgently required. It was clear, however, that this could not be delayed; and Zebek-Dorchi took the task willingly upon himself. But where or how should this notification be made, so as to exclude Russian hearers? After some deliberation the following plan was adopted: Couriers, it was contrived, should arrive in furious haste, one upon the heels of another, reporting a sudden inroad of the Kirghizes and Bashkirs upon the Kalmuck lands at a point distant about one hundred and twenty miles. Thither all the Kalmuck families, according to immemorial custom, were required to send a separate representative; and there, accordingly, within three days, all appeared. The distance, the solitary ground appointed for the rendezvous, the rapidity of the march, all tended to make it almost certain that no Russian could be present. Zebek-Dorchi then came forward. He did not waste many words upon rhetoric. He unfurled an immense sheet of parchment, visible from the outermost distance at which any of this vast crowd could stand. The total number amounted to eighty thousand: all saw, and many heard. They were told of the oppressions of Russia; of her pride and haughty disdain, evidenced towards them by a thousand acts; of her contempt for their religion; of her determination to reduce them to absolute slavery; of the preliminary measures she had already taken by erecting forts upon many of the great rivers of their neighborhood; of the ulterior intentions she thus announced to circumscribe their pastoral lands, until they would all be obliged to renounce their flocks and to collect in towns like Sarepta, there to pursue mechanical and servile trades of shoemaker, tailor, and weaver, such as the freeborn Tartar had always disdained. "Then, again," said the subtle prince, "she increases her military levies upon our population every year. We pour out our blood as young men in her defence, or more often in support of her insolent aggressions; and as old men we reap nothing from our sufferings, nor benefit by our survivorship where so many are sacrificed." At this point of his harangue, Zebek produced several papers (forged, as it is generally believed, by himself and the lama) containing projects of the Russian court for a general transfer of the eldest sons, taken *en masse* from the greatest Kalmuck families, to the imperial court. "Now, let this be once accomplished," he argued, "and there is an end of all useful resistance from that day forwards. Petitions we might make, or even remonstrances; as men of words, we might play a bold part: but for deeds, for that sort of language by which our ancestors were used to speak, holding us by such a chain, Russia would make a jest of our wishes, knowing full well that we should not dare to make any effectual movement."

Having thus sufficiently roused the angry passions of his vast audience, and having alarmed their fears by this pretended scheme against their firstborn (an artifice which was indispensable to his purpose, because it met beforehand *every* form of amendment to his proposal coming from the more moderate nobles, who would not otherwise have failed to insist upon trying the effect of bold addresses to the empress before resorting to any desperate extremity), Zebek-Dorchi opened his scheme of revolt, and, if so, of instant revolt; since any preparations reported at St. Petersburg would be a signal for the armies of Russia to cross into such positions from all parts of Asia as would effectually intercept their march. It is remarkable, however, that, with all his audacity and his reliance upon the momentary excitement of the Kalmucks, the subtle prince did not venture at this stage of his seduction to make so startling a proposal as that of a flight to China. All that he held out for the present was a rapid march to the Temba or some other great river, which they were to cross, and to take up a strong position on the farther bank, from which, as from a post of conscious security, they could hold a bolder language to the Czarina, and one which would have a better chance of winning a favorable audience.

These things, in the irritated condition of the simple Tartars, passed by acclamation; and all returned homewards to push forward with the most furious speed the preparations for their awful undertaking. Rapid and energetic these of necessity were; and in that degree they became noticeable and manifest to the Russians who happened to be intermingled with the different hordes, either on commercial errands or as agents officially from the Russian government,— some in a financial, others in a diplomatic character.

Among these last (indeed, at the head of them) was a Russian of some distinction, by name Kichinskoi, a man memorable for his vanity, and memorable also as one of the many victims to the Tartar revolution. This Kichinskoi had been sent by the empress as her envoy to overlook the conduct of the Kalmucks. He was styled the *grand pristaw*, or great commissioner, and was universally known among the Tartar tribes by this title. His mixed character of ambassador and of political *surveillant*, combined with the dependent state of the Kalmucks, gave him a real weight in the Tartar councils, and might have given him a far greater had not his outrageous self-conceit and his arrogant confidence in his own authority, as due chiefly to his personal qualities for command, led him into such harsh displays of power and menaces so odious to the Tartar pride as very soon made him an object of their profoundest malice. He had publicly insulted the khan; and upon making a communication to him to the effect that some reports began to circulate, and even to reach the empress, of a design in agitation to fly from the imperial dominions, he had ventured to say, "But this you dare not attempt. I laugh at such rumors: yes, khan, I laugh at them to the empress; for you are a chained bear, and that you know." The khan turned away on his heel with marked disdain; and the pristaw, foaming at the mouth, continued to utter, amongst those of the khan's attendants who stayed behind to catch his real sentiments in a moment of unguarded passion, all that the blindest frenzy of rage could suggest to the most presumptuous of fools. It was now ascertained that suspicions *had* arisen; but at the same time it was ascertained that the pristaw spoke no more than the truth in representing himself to have discredited these suspicions. The fact was, that the mere infatuation of vanity made him believe that nothing could go on undetected by his all-piercing sagacity, and that no rebellion could prosper when rebuked by his commanding presence. The Tartars, therefore, pursued their preparations, confiding in the obstinate blindness of the grand pristaw, as in their perfect safeguard; and such it proved, to his own ruin as well as that of myriads beside.

Christmas arrived; and a little before that time courier upon courier came dropping in, one upon the very heels of another, to St. Petersburg, assuring the Czarina that beyond all doubt the Kalmucks were in the very crisis of departure. These despatches came from the governor of Astrakhan; and copies were instantly forwarded to Kichinskoi. Now, it happened that between this governor, a Russian named Beketoff, and the pristaw, had been an ancient feud. The very name of Beketoff inflamed his resentment; and no sooner did he see that hated name attached to the despatch than he felt himself confirmed in his former views with tenfold bigotry, and wrote instantly, in terms of the most pointed ridicule, against the new alarmist, pledging his own head upon the visionariness of his alarms. Beketoff, however, was not to be put down by a few hard words or by ridicule. He persisted in his statements. The Russian ministry were confounded by the obstinacy of the disputants; and some were beginning even to treat the governor of Astrakhan as a bore and as the dupe of his own nervous terrors, when the memorable day arrived, the fatal 5th of January, which forever terminated the dispute, and put a seal upon the earthly hopes and fortunes of unnumbered myriads. The governor of Astrakhan was the first to hear the news. Stung by the mixed furies of jealousy, of triumphant vengeance, and of anxious ambition, he sprang into his sledge, and at the rate of three hundred miles a day pursued his route to St. Petersburg, rushed into the imperial presence, announced the total realization of his worst predictions, and upon the confirmation of this intelligence by subsequent despatches from many different posts on the Wolga, he received an imperial commission to seize the person of his deluded enemy and to keep him in strict captivity. These orders were eagerly fulfilled; and the unfortunate Kichinskoi soon afterward expired of grief and mortification in the gloomy solitude of a dungeon, — a victim to his own immeasurable vanity and the blinding self-delusions of a presumption that refused all warning.

The governor of Astrakhan had been but too faithful a prophet. Perhaps even *he* was surprised at the suddenness with which the verification followed his reports. Precisely on the 5th of January, the day so solemnly appointed under religious sanctions by the lama, the Kalmucks on the east bank of the Wolga were seen at the earliest dawn of day assembling by troops and squadrons, and in the tumultuous movement of some great morning of battle. Tens of thousands continued moving off the ground at every half hour's interval. Women and children, to the amount of two hundred thousand and upwards, were placed upon wagons or upon camels, and drew off by masses of twenty thousand at once, placed under suitable escorts, and continually swelled in numbers by other outlying bodies of the horde who kept falling in at various distances upon the first and the second day's march. From sixty to eighty thousand of those who were the best mounted stayed behind the rest of the tribes, with purposes of devastation and plunder more violent than prudence justified or the amiable character of the khan could be supposed to approve. But in this, as in other instances, he was completely overruled by the malignant counsels of Zebek-Dorchi. The first tempest of the desolating fury of the Tartars discharged itself upon their own habitations. But this, as cutting off all infirm looking backward from the hardships of their march, had been thought so necessary a measure by all the chieftains, that even Oubacha himself was the first to authorize the act by his own example. He seized a torch, previously prepared with materials the most durable as well as combustible, and steadily applied it to the timbers of his own palace. Nothing was saved from the general wreck except the portable part of the domestic utensils and that part of the woodwork which could be applied to the manufacture of the long Tartar lances. This chapter in their memorable day's work being finished, and the whole of their villages throughout a district of ten thousand square miles in one simultaneous blaze, the Tartars waited for further orders.

These, it was intended, should have taken a character of valedictory vengeance, and thus have left behind to the Czarina a dreadful commentary upon the main motives of their flight. It was the purpose of Zebek-Dorchi that all the Russian towns, churches, and buildings of every description should be given up to pillage and destruction, and such treatment applied to the defenceless inhabitants as might naturally be expected from a fierce people already infuriated by the spectacle of their own outrages and by the bloody retaliations which they must necessarily have provoked. This part of the tragedy, however, was happily intercepted by a providential disappointment at the very crisis of departure. It has been mentioned already that the motive for selecting the depth of winter as the season of flight (which otherwise was obviously the very worst possible) had been the impossibility of effecting a junction sufficiently rapid with the tribes on the west of the Wolga, in the absence of bridges, unless by a natural bridge of ice. For this one advantage the Kalmuck leaders had consented to aggravate by a thousandfold the calamities inevitable to a rapid flight over boundless tracts of country with women, children, and herds of cattle,— for this one single advantage; and yet, after all, it was lost. The reason never has been explained satisfactorily; but the fact was such. Some have said that the signals were not properly concerted for marking the moment of absolute departure; that is, for signifying whether the settled intention of the eastern Kalmucks might not have been suddenly interrupted by adverse intelligence. Others have supposed that the ice might not be equally strong on both sides of the river, and might even be generally insecure for the treading of heavy and heavily laden animals such as camels. But the prevailing notion is, that some accidental movements, on the 3d and 4th of January, of Russian troops in the neighborhood of the western Kalmucks, though really having no reference to them or their plans, had been construed into certain signs that all was discovered, and that the prudence of the western chieftains, who, from situation, had never been exposed to those intrigues by which Zebek-Dorchi had practised upon the pride of the eastern tribes, now stepped in to save their people from ruin. Be the cause what it might, it is certain that the western Kalmucks were in some way prevented from forming the intended junction with their brethren of the opposite bank; and the result was, that at least one hundred thousand of these Tartars were

left behind in Russia. This accident it was which saved
their Russian neighbors universally from the desolation
which else awaited them. One general massacre and conflagration would assuredly have surprised them, to the utter
extermination of their property, their houses, and themselves, had it not been for this disappointment. But the
eastern chieftains did not dare to put to hazard the safety
of their brethren under the first impulse of the Czarina's
vengeance for so dreadful a tragedy; for, as they were well
aware of too many circumstances by which she might dis-
cover the concurrence of the western people in the general
scheme of revolt, they justly feared that she would thence
infer their concurrence also in the bloody events which
marked its outset.

Little did the western Kalmucks guess what reasons they
also had for gratitude on account of an interposition so
unexpected, and which, at the moment, they so generally
deplored. Could they but have witnessed the thousandth
part of the sufferings which overtook their eastern brethren
in the first month of their sad flight, they would have
blessed Heaven for their own narrow escape; and yet these
sufferings of the first month were but a prelude or foretaste
comparatively slight of those which afterwards succeeded.

For now began to unroll the most awful series of calamities, and the most extensive, which is anywhere recorded
to have visited the sons and daughters of men. It is possible that the sudden inroads of destroying nations — such
as the Huns, or the Avars, or the Mongol Tartars — may
have inflicted misery as extensive; but there the misery
and the desolation would be sudden, like the flight of volleying lightning. Those who were spared at first would
generally be spared to the end; those who perished would
perish instantly. It is possible that the French retreat
from Moscow may have made some nearer approach to this
calamity in duration, though still a feeble and miniature

approach, for the French sufferings did not commence in good earnest until about one month from the time of leaving Moscow; and though it is true that afterwards the vials of wrath were emptied upon the devoted army for six or seven weeks in succession, yet what is that to this Kalmuck tragedy, which lasted for more than as many months? But the main feature of horror, by which the Tartar march was distinguished from the French, lies in the accompaniment of women and children. There were both, it is true, with the French army, but so few as to bear no visible proportion to the total numbers concerned. The French, in short, were merely an army,— a host of professional destroyers, whose regular trade was bloodshed, and whose regular element was danger and suffering. But the Tartars were a nation carrying along with them more than two hundred and fifty thousand women and children, utterly unequal, for the most part, to any contest with the calamities before them. The children of Israel were in the same circumstances as to the accompaniment of their families; but they were released from the pursuit of their enemies in a very early stage of their flight; and their subsequent residence in the desert was not a march, but a continued halt, and under a continued interposition of Heaven for their comfortable support. Earthquakes, again, however comprehensive in their ravages, are shocks of a moment's duration. A much nearer approach made to the wide range and the long duration of the Kalmuck tragedy may have been in a pestilence such as that which visited Athens in the Peloponnesian War, or London in the reign of Charles II. There, also, the martyrs were counted by myriads, and the period of the desolation was counted by months. But, after all, the total amount of destruction was on a smaller scale; and there was this feature of alleviation to the *conscious* pressure of the calamity, — that the misery was withdrawn from public notice into private chambers and hospitals. The siege of Jerusalem by Vespasian and his son, taken in its entire circumstances, comes nearest of all for breadth and depth of suffering, for duration, for the exasperation of the suffering from without by internal feuds, and, finally, for that last most appalling expression of the furnace heat of the anguish in its power to extinguish the natural affections even of maternal love. But, after all, each case had circumstances of romantic misery peculiar to itself,—circumstances without precedent, and (wherever human nature is ennobled by Christianity), it may be confidently hoped, never to be repeated.

The first point to be reached, before any hope of repose could be encouraged, was the river Jaik. This was not above three hundred miles from the main point of departure on the Wolga; and, if the march thither was to be a forced one and a severe one, it was alleged, on the other hand, that the suffering would be the more brief and transient: one summary exertion, not to be repeated, and all was achieved. Forced the march was, and severe beyond example,—there the forewarning proved correct,—but the promised rest proved a mere phantom of the wilderness, a visionary rainbow, which fled before their hope-sick eyes, across these interminable solitudes, for seven months of hardship and calamity, without a pause. These sufferings, by their very nature and the circumstances under which they arose, were (like the scenery of the steppes) somewhat monotonous in their coloring and external features. What variety, however, there was, will be most naturally exhibited by tracing historically the successive stages of the general misery exactly as it unfolded itself under the double agency of weakness, still increasing from within, and hostile pressure from without. Viewed in this manner, under the real order of development, it is remarkable that these sufferings of the Tartars, though under the moulding hands of accident, arrange themselves almost with a scenical propriety.

They seem combined as with the skill of an artist, the intensity of the misery advancing regularly with the advances of the march, and the stages of the calamity corresponding to the stages of the route; so that, upon raising the curtain which veils the great catastrophe, we behold one vast climax of anguish, towering upwards by regular gradations, as if constructed artificially for picturesque effect,—a result which might not have been surprising, had it been reasonable to anticipate the same rate of speed, and even an accelerated rate, as prevailing through the later stages of the expedition. But it seemed, on the contrary, most reasonable to calculate upon a continual decrement in the rate of motion according to the increasing distance from the headquarters of the pursuing enemy. This calculation, however, was defeated by the extraordinary circumstance that the Russian armies did not begin to close in very fiercely upon the Kalmucks until after they had accomplished a distance of full two thousand miles. One thousand miles farther on, the assaults became even more tumultuous and murderous; and already the great shadows of the Chinese Wall were dimly descried, when the frenzy and *acharnement* of the pursuers and the bloody desperation of the miserable fugitives had reached its uttermost extremity. Let us briefly rehearse the main stages of the misery, and trace the ascending steps of the tragedy according to the great divisions of the route marked out by the central rivers of Asia.

The first stage, we have already said, was from the Wolga to the Jaik; the distance about three hundred miles; the time allowed seven days. For the first week, therefore, the rate of marching averaged about forty-three English miles a day. The weather was cold but bracing; and at a more moderate pace this part of the journey might have been accomplished without much distress by a people as hardy as the Kalmucks. As it was, the cattle suffered greatly from overdriving; milk began to fail even for the children; the sheep perished by wholesale; and the children themselves were saved only by the innumerable camels.

The Cossacks who dwelt upon the banks of the Jaik were the first among the subjects of Russia to come into collision with the Kalmucks. Great was their surprise at the suddenness of the irruption, and great, also, their consternation; for, according to their settled custom, by far the greater part of their number was absent during the winter months at the fisheries upon the Caspian. Some who were liable to surprise at the most exposed points fled in crowds to the fortress of Koulagina, which was immediately invested and summoned by Oubacha. He had, however, in his train only a few light pieces of artillery; and the Russian commandant at Koulagina, being aware of the hurried circumstances in which the khan was placed, and that he stood upon the very edge, as it were, of a renewed flight, felt encouraged by these considerations to a more obstinate resistance than might else have been advisable with an enemy so little disposed to observe the usages of civilized warfare. The period of his anxiety was not long. On the fifth day of the siege he descried from the walls a succession of Tartar couriers, mounted upon fleet Bactrian camels, crossing the vast plains around the fortress at a furious pace, and riding into the Kalmuck encampment at various points. Great agitation appeared immediately to follow. Orders were soon after despatched in all directions; and it became speedily known that upon a distant flank of the Kalmuck movement a bloody and exterminating battle had been fought the day before, in which one entire tribe of the khan's dependents, numbering not less than nine thousand fighting men, had perished to the last man. This was the *ouloss*, or clan, called *Feka-Zechorr*, between whom and the Cossacks there was a feud of ancient standing. In selecting, therefore, the points of attack, on occasion of the present hasty inroad, the Cossack chiefs were naturally eager so to direct their efforts as to combine with the service of the empress some gratification to their own party hatreds, more especially as the present was likely to be their final opportunity for revenge, if the Kalmuck evasion should prosper. Having, therefore, concentrated as large a body of Cossack cavalry as circumstances allowed, they attacked the hostile *ouloss* with a precipitation which denied to it all means for communicating with Oubacha; for the necessity of commanding an ample range of pasturage, to meet the necessities of their vast flocks and herds, had separated this *ouloss* from the khan's headquarters by an interval of eighty miles: and thus it was, and not from oversight, that it came to be thrown entirely upon its own resources. These had proved insufficient. Retreat, from the exhausted state of their horses and camels, no less than from the prodigious incumbrances of their live stock, was absolutely out of the question. Quarter was disdained on the one side, and would not have been granted on the other; and thus it had happened that the setting sun of that one day (the thirteenth from the first opening of the revolt) threw his parting rays upon the final agonies of an ancient *ouloss*, stretched upon a bloody field, who on that day's dawning had held and styled themselves an independent nation.

Universal consternation was diffused through the wide borders of the khan's encampment by this disastrous intelligence, not so much on account of the numbers slain, or the total extinction of a powerful ally, as because the position of the Cossack force was likely to put to hazard the future advances of the Kalmucks, or at least to retard and hold them in check until the heavier columns of the Russian army should arrive upon their flanks. The siege of Koulagina was instantly raised; and that signal, so fatal to the happiness of the women and children, once again

resounded through the tents,— the signal for flight, and
this time for a flight more rapid than ever. About one
hundred and fifty miles ahead of their present position
there arose a tract of hilly country, forming a sort of margin to the vast, sealike expanse of champaign savannas,
steppes, and occasionally of sandy deserts, which stretched
away on each side of this margin both eastwards and west-
wards. Pretty nearly in the centre of this hilly range lay
a narrow defile, through which passed the nearest and the
most practicable route to the river Torgau (the farther bank
of which river offered the next great station of security for
a general halt). It was the more essential to gain this pass
before the Cossacks, inasmuch as not only would the delay
in forcing the pass give time to the Russian pursuing
columns for combining their attacks and for bringing up
their artillery, but also because (even if all enemies in pursuit were thrown out of the question) it was held by those
best acquainted with the difficult and obscure geography of
these pathless steppes that the loss of this one narrow strait
amongst the hills would have the effect of throwing them
(as their only alternative in a case where so wide a sweep of
pasturage was required) upon a circuit of at least five hundred miles extra; besides that, after all, this circuitous
route would carry them to the Torgau at a point ill fitted for
the passage of their heavy baggage. The defile in the hills,
therefore, it was resolved to gain; and yet, unless they
moved upon it with the velocity of light cavalry, there was
little chance but it would be found preoccupied by the Cossacks. They, it is true, had suffered greatly in the recent
sanguinary action with their enemies; but the excitement
of victory, and the intense sympathy with their unexam-
pled triumph, had again swelled their ranks, and would
probably act with the force of a vortex to draw in their
simple countrymen from the Caspian. The question, therefore, of preoccupation was reduced to a race. The Cossacks

were marching upon an oblique line not above fifty miles longer than that which led to the same point from the Kalmuck headquarters before Koulagina; and therefore, without the most furious haste on the part of the Kalmucks, there was not a chance for them, burdened and "trashed" as they were, to anticipate so agile a light cavalry as the Cossacks in seizing this important pass.

Dreadful were the feelings of the poor women on hearing this exposition of the case; for they easily understood that too capital an interest (the *summa rerum*) was now at stake to allow of any regard to minor interests, or what would be considered such in their present circumstances. The dreadful week already passed — their inauguration in misery — was yet fresh in their remembrance. The scars of suffering were impressed not only upon their memories, but upon their very persons and the persons of their children; and they knew that, where no speed had much chance of meeting the cravings of the chieftains, no test would be accepted, short of absolute exhaustion, that as much had been accomplished as could be accomplished. Weseloff, the Russian captive, has recorded the silent wretchedness with which the women and elder boys assisted in drawing the tent ropes. On the 5th of January all had been animation and the joyousness of indefinite expectation; now, on the contrary, a brief but bitter experience had taught them to take an amended calculation of what it was that lay before them.

One whole day, and far into the succeeding night, had the renewed flight continued. The sufferings had been greater than before; for the cold had been more intense, and many perished out of the living creatures through every class except only the camels, whose powers of endurance seemed equally adapted to cold and heat. The second morning, however, brought an alleviation to the distress. Snow had begun to fall; and, though not deep at present, it was easily foreseen that it soon would be so, and that, as a halt would in that case become unavoidable, no plan could be better than that of staying where they were, especially as the same cause would check the advance of the Cossacks. Here, then, was the last interval of comfort which gleamed upon the unhappy nation during their whole migration. For ten days the snow continued to fall with little intermission. At the end of that time, keen, bright, frosty weather succeeded: the drifting had ceased. In three days the smooth expanse became firm enough to support the treading of the camels, and the flight was recommenced. But during the halt much domestic comfort had been enjoyed, and, for the last time, universal plenty. The cows and oxen had perished in such vast numbers on the previous marches, that an order was now issued to turn what remained to account by slaughtering the whole, and salting whatever part should be found to exceed the immediate consumption. This measure led to a scene of general banqueting, and even of festivity, amongst all who were not incapacitated for joyous emotions by distress of mind, by grief for the unhappy experience of the few last days, and by anxiety for the too gloomy future. Seventy thousand persons of all ages had already perished, exclusive of the many thousand allies who had been cut down by the Cossack sabre; and the losses in reversion were likely to be many more. For rumors began now to arrive from all quarters, by the mounted couriers whom the khan had despatched to the rear and to each flank as well as in advance, that large masses of the imperial troops were converging from all parts of Central Asia to the fords of the river Torgau, as the most convenient point for intercepting the flying tribes; and it was by this time well known that a powerful division was close in their rear, and was retarded only by the numerous artillery which had been judged necessary to support their operations. New motives were thus daily arising for quickening the motions of the wretched

Kalmucks and for exhausting those who were previously but too much exhausted.

It was not until the second day of February that the khan's advanced guard came in sight of Ouchim, the defile among the hills of Moulgaldchares, in which they anticipated so bloody an opposition from the Cossacks. A pretty large body of these light cavalry had, in fact, preoccupied the pass by some hours; but the khan, having two great advantages,— namely, a strong body of infantry, who had been conveyed by sections of five on about two hundred camels, and some pieces of light artillery which he had not yet been forced to abandon,— soon began to make a serious impression upon this unsupported detachment, and they would probably at any rate have retired; but at the very moment when they were making some dispositions in that view Zebek-Dorchi appeared upon their rear with a body of trained riflemen who had distinguished themselves in the war with Turkey. These men had contrived to crawl unobserved over the cliffs which skirted the ravine, availing themselves of the dry beds of the summer torrents, and other inequalities of the ground, to conceal their movement. Disorder and trepidation ensued instantly in the Cossack files. The khan, who had been waiting with the *élite* of his heavy cavalry, charged furiously upon them. Total overthrow followed to the Cossacks, and a slaughter such as in some measure avenged the recent bloody extermination of their allies, the ancient *ouloss* of Feka-Zechorr. The slight horses of the Cossacks were unable to support the weight of heavy Polish dragoons and a body of trained *cameleers* (that is, cuirassiers mounted on camels). Hardy they were, but not strong, nor a match for their antagonists in weight; and their extraordinary efforts through the last few days to gain their present position had greatly diminished their powers for effecting an escape. Very few, in fact, *did* escape; and the bloody day of Ouchim became as memorable among the Cossacks as that which, about twenty days before, had signalized the complete annihilation of the Feka-Zechorr.

The road was now open to the river Igritch, and as yet even far beyond it to the Torgau; but how long this state of things would continue was every day more doubtful. Certain intelligence was now received that a large Russian army, well appointed in every arm, was advancing upon the Torgau under the command of General Traubenberg. This officer was to be joined on his route by ten thousand Bashkirs and pretty nearly the same amount of Kirghizes,— both hereditary enemies of the Kalmucks, both exasperated to a point of madness by the bloody trophies which Oubacha and Momotbacha had in late years won from such of their compatriots as served under the Sultan. The Czarina's yoke these wild nations bore with submissive patience, but not the hands by which it had been imposed; and accordingly, catching with eagerness at the present occasion offered to their vengeance, they sent an assurance to the Czarina of their perfect obedience to her commands, and at the same time a message significantly declaring in what spirit they meant to execute them, namely, "that they would not trouble her Majesty with prisoners."

Here then arose, as before with the Cossacks, a race for the Kalmucks with the regular armies of Russia, and concurrently with nations as fierce and semi-humanized as themselves, besides that they were stung into threefold activity by the furies of mortified pride and military abasement under the eyes of the Turkish Sultan. The forces, and more especially the artillery, of Russia were far too overwhelming to permit the thought of a regular opposition in pitched battles, even with a less dilapidated state of their resources than they could reasonably expect at the period of their arrival on the Torgau. In their speed lay their only hope,— in strength of foot, as before, and not in strength of arm. Onward, therefore, the Kalmucks pressed, marking the lines of their wide-extending march over the sad solitudes of the steppes by a never-ending chain of corpses. The old and the young, the sick man on his couch, the mother with her baby,—all were left behind. Sights such as these, with the many rueful aggravations incident to the helpless condition of infancy,—of disease and of female weakness abandoned to the wolves amidst a howling wilderness,—continued to track their course through a space of full two thousand miles; for so much at the least it was likely to prove, including the circuits to which they were often compelled by rivers or hostile tribes, from the point of starting on the Wolga until they could reach their destined halting ground on the east bank of the Torgau. For the first seven weeks of this march their sufferings had been embittered by the excessive severity of the cold; and every night—so long as wood was to be had for fires, either from the lading of the camels, or from the desperate sacrifice of their baggage wagons, or (as occasionally happened) from the forests which skirted the banks of the many rivers which crossed their path—no spectacle was more frequent than that of a circle, composed of men, women, and children, gathered by hundreds round a central fire, all dead and stiff at the return of morning light. Myriads were left behind from pure exhaustion, of whom none had a chance, under the combined evils which beset them, of surviving through the next twenty-four hours. Frost, however, and snow at length ceased to persecute; the vast extent of the march at length brought them into more genial latitudes; and the unusual duration of the march was gradually bringing them into the more genial seasons of the year. Two thousand miles had at least been traversed; February, March, April, were gone; the balmy month of May had opened; vernal sights and sounds came from every side to comfort the heart-weary travellers; and at last, in the latter end of May, they crossed the Torgau, and took up a position where they hoped to find liberty to repose themselves for many weeks in comfort as well as in security, and to draw such supplies from the fertile neighborhood as might restore their shattered forces to a condition for executing, with less of wreck and ruin, the large remainder of the journey.

Yes, it was true that two thousand miles of wandering had been completed, but in a period of nearly five months, and with the terrific sacrifice of at least two hundred and fifty thousand souls, to say nothing of herds and flocks past all reckoning. These had all perished, — ox, cow, horse, mule, ass, sheep, or goat: not one survived, — only the camels. These arid and adust creatures, looking like the mummies of some antediluvian animals, without the affections or sensibilities of flesh and blood, — these only still erected their speaking eyes to the eastern heavens, and had to all appearance come out from this long tempest of trial unscathed and unharmed. The khan, knowing how much he was individually answerable for the misery which had been sustained, must have wept tears even more bitter than those of Xerxes when he threw his eyes over the myriads whom he had assembled; for the tears of Xerxes were unmingled with compunction. Whatever amends were in his power he resolved to make by sacrifices to the general good of all personal regards; and accordingly, even at this point of their advance, he once more deliberately brought under review the whole question of the revolt. The question was formally debated before the council, whether, even at this point, they should untread their steps, and, throwing themselves upon the Czarina's mercy, return to their old allegiance. In that case, Oubacha professed himself willing to become the scapegoat for the general transgression. This, he argued, was no fantastic scheme, but even easy of accomplishment; for the unlimited and sacred power of the khan, so well known to the empress, made it absolutely iniquitous to attribute any separate responsibility to the people. Upon the khan rested the guilt; upon the khan would descend the imperial vengeance. This proposal was applauded for its generosity, but was energetically opposed by Zebek-Dorchi. Were they to lose the whole journey of two thousand miles? Was their misery to perish without fruit? True it was that they had yet reached only the halfway house; but in that respect the motives were evenly balanced for retreat or for advance. Either way they would have pretty nearly the same distance to traverse, but with this difference,— that, forwards, their route lay through lands comparatively fertile; backwards through a blasted wilderness, rich only in memorials of their sorrow, and hideous to Kalmuck eyes by the trophies of their calamity. Besides, though the empress might accept an excuse for the past, would she the less forbear to suspect for the future? The Czarina's *pardon* they might obtain; but could they ever hope to recover her *confidence?* Doubtless there would now be a standing presumption against them, an immortal ground of jealousy; and a jealous government would be but another name for a harsh one. Finally, whatever motives there ever had been for the revolt surely remained unimpaired by anything that had occurred. In reality the revolt was, after all, no revolt, but (strictly speaking) a return to their old allegiance; since not above one hundred and fifty years ago (*viz.*, in the year 1616), their ancestors had revolted from the Emperor of China. They had now tried both governments; and for them China was the land of promise, and Russia the house of bondage.

Spite, however, of all that Zebek could say or do, the yearning of the people was strongly in behalf of the khan's proposal; the pardon of their prince, they persuaded themselves, would be readily conceded by the empress; and

there is little doubt that they would at this time have
thrown themselves gladly upon the imperial mercy,— when
suddenly all was defeated by the arrival of two envoys from
Traubenberg. This general had reached the fortress of
Orsk, after a very painful march, on the 12th of April;
thence he set forwards towards Oriembourg, which he
reached upon the 1st of June, having been joined on his
route, at various times through the month of May, by the
Kirghizes and a corps of ten thousand Bashkirs. From
Oriembourg he sent forward his official offers to the khan,
which were harsh and peremptory, holding out no specific
stipulations as to pardon or impunity, and exacting uncon-
ditional submission as the preliminary price of any cessa-
tion from military operations. The personal character of
Traubenberg, which was anything but energetic, and the
condition of his army, disorganized in a great measure by
the length and severity of the march, made it probable,
that, with a little time for negotiation, a more conciliatory
tone would have been assumed. But, unhappily for all
parties, sinister events occurred in the meantime, such as
effectually put an end to every hope of the kind.

The two envoys sent forward by Traubenberg had reported to this officer that a distance of only ten days' march
lay between his own headquarters and those of the khan.
Upon this fact transpiring, the Kirghizes, by their prince
Nourali, and the Bashkirs, entreated the Russian general
to advance without delay. Once having placed his cannon
in position, so as to command the Kalmuck camp, the fate
of the rebel khan and his people would be in his own hands,
and they would themselves form his advanced guard. Traubenberg, however,— *why* has not been certainly explained,
— refused to march, grounding his refusal upon the condition of his army and their absolute need of refreshment.
Long and fierce was the altercation; but at length, seeing
no chance of prevailing, and dreading above all other events

the escape of their detested enemy, the ferocious Bashkirs went off in a body by forced marches. In six days they reached the Torgau, crossed by swimming their horses, and fell upon the Kalmucks, who were dispersed for many a league in search of food or provender for their camels. The first day's action was one vast succession of independent skirmishes diffused over a field of thirty to forty miles in extent; one party often breaking up into three or four, and again (according to the accidents of ground), three or four blending into one; flight and pursuit, rescue and total overthrow, going on simultaneously, under all varieties of form, in all quarters of the plain. The Bashkirs had found themselves obliged, by the scattered state of the Kalmucks, to split up into innumerable sections; and thus, for some hours, it had been impossible for the most practised eye to collect the general tendency of the day's fortune. Both the khan and Zebek-Dorchi were at one moment made prisoners, and more than once in imminent danger of being cut down; but at length Zebek succeeded in rallying a strong column of infantry, which, with the support of the camel corps on each flank, compelled the Bashkirs to retreat. Clouds, however, of these wild cavalry continued to arrive through the next two days and nights, followed or accompanied by the Kirghizes. These being viewed as the advanced parties of Traubenberg's army, the Kalmuck chieftains saw no hope of safety but in flight; and in this way it happened that a retreat which had so recently been brought to a pause, was resumed at the very moment when the unhappy fugitives were anticipating a deep repose, without further molestation, the whole summer through.

It seemed as though every variety of wretchedness were predestined to the Kalmucks, and as if their sufferings were incomplete unless they were rounded and matured by all that the most dreadful agencies of summer's heat could superadd to those of frost and winter. To this sequel of their story we shall immediately revert, after first noticing a little romantic episode which occurred at this point between Oubacha and his unprincipled cousin Zebek-Dorchi.

There was, at the time of the Kalmuck flight from the Wolga, a Russian gentleman of some rank at the court of the khan, whom for political reasons it was thought necessary to carry along with them as a captive. For some weeks his confinement had been very strict, and in one or two instances cruel. But as the increasing distance was continually diminishing the chances of escape, and perhaps, also, as the misery of the guards gradually withdrew their attention from all minor interests to their own personal sufferings, the vigilance of the custody grew more and more relaxed, until at length, upon a petition to the khan, Mr. Weseloff was formally restored to liberty; and it was understood that he might use his liberty in whatever way he chose, even for returning to Russia, if that should be his wish. Accordingly, he was making active preparations for his journey to St. Petersburg, when it occurred to Zebek-Dorchi that not improbably, in some of the battles which were then anticipated with Traubenberg, it might happen to them to lose some prisoner of rank, in which case the Russian Weseloff would be a pledge in their hands for negotiating an exchange. Upon this plea, to his own severe affliction, the Russian was detained until the further pleasure of the khan. The khan's name, indeed, was used through the whole affair, but, as it seemed, with so little concurrence on his part, that when Weseloff in a private audience humbly remonstrated upon the injustice done him, and the cruelty of thus sporting with his feelings by setting him at liberty, and, as it were, tempting him into dreams of home and restored happiness, only for the purpose of blighting them, the good-natured prince disclaimed all participation in the affair, and went so far in proving his sincerity as even to give him permission to effect his escape;

and, as a ready means of commencing it without raising suspicion, the khan mentioned to Mr. Weseloff that he had just then received a message from the hetman of the Bashkirs, soliciting a private interview on the banks of the Torgau at a spot pointed out. That interview was arranged for the coming night; and Mr. Weseloff might go in the khan's suite, which on either side was not to exceed three persons. Weseloff was a prudent man, acquainted with the world, and he read treachery in the very outline of this scheme as stated by the khan, — treachery against the khan's person. He mused a little, and then communicated so much of his suspicions to the khan as might put him on his guard; but, upon further consideration, he begged leave to decline the honor of accompanying the khan. The fact was, that three Kalmucks, who had strong motives for returning to their countrymen on the west bank of the Wolga, guessing the intentions of Weseloff, had offered to join him in his escape. These men the khan would probably find himself obliged to countenance in their project; so that it became a point of honor with Weseloff to conceal their intentions, and therefore to accomplish the evasion from the camp (of which the first step only would be hazardous) without risking the notice of the khan.

The district in which they were now encamped abounded through many hundred miles with wild horses of a docile and beautiful breed. Each of the four fugitives had caught from seven to ten of these spirited creatures in the course of the last few days. This raised no suspicion; for the rest of the Kalmucks had been making the same sort of provision against the coming toils of their remaining route to China. These horses were secured by halters, and hidden about dusk in the thickets which lined the margin of the river. To these thickets, about ten at night, the four fugitives repaired. They took a circuitous path which drew them as little as possible within danger of challenge from any of the outposts or of the patrols which had been established on the quarters where the Bashkirs lay, and in three quarters of an hour they reached the rendezvous. The moon had now risen, the horses were unfastened, and they were in the act of mounting, when the deep silence of the woods was disturbed by a violent uproar and the clashing of arms. Weseloff fancied that he heard the voice of the khan shouting for assistance. He remembered the communication made by that prince in the morning, and, requesting his companions to support him, he rode off in the direction of the sound. A very short distance brought him to an open glade in the wood, where he beheld four men contending with a party of at least nine or ten. Two of the four were dismounted at the very instant of Weseloff's arrival. One of these he recognized almost certainly as the khan, who was fighting hand to hand, but at great disadvantage, with two of the adverse horsemen. Seeing that no time was to be lost, Weseloff fired, and brought down one of the two. His companions discharged their carbines at the same moment, and then all rushed simultaneously into the little open area. The thundering sound of about thirty horses, all rushing at once into a narrow space, gave the impression that a whole troop of cavalry was coming down upon the assailants, who accordingly wheeled about and fled with one impulse. Weseloff advanced to the dismounted cavalier, who, as he expected, proved to be the khan. The man whom Weseloff had shot was lying dead; and both were shocked, though Weseloff at least was not surprised, on stooping down, and scrutinizing his features, to recognize a well-known confidential servant of Zebek-Dorchi. Nothing was said by either party. The khan rode off, escorted by Weseloff and his companions; and for some time a dead silence prevailed. The situation of Weseloff was delicate and critical. To leave the khan at this point was probably to cancel their recent services; for he might be again crossed on his path, and again attacked by the very party from whom he had just been delivered. Yet, on the other hand, to return to the camp was to endanger the chances of accomplishing the escape. The khan, also, was apparently revolving all this in his mind; for at length he broke silence, and said, "I comprehend your situation, and under other circumstances I might feel it my duty to detain your companions; but it would ill become me to do so after the important service you have just rendered me. Let us turn a little to the left. There, where you see the watchfire, is an outpost. Attend me so far. I am then safe. You may turn, and pursue your enterprise; for the circumstances under which you will appear, as my escort, are sufficient to shield you from all suspicion for the present. I regret having no better means at my disposal for testifying my gratitude. But tell me, before we part, — Was it accident only which led you to my rescue? Or had you acquired any knowledge of the plot by which I was decoyed into this snare?" Weseloff answered very candidly that mere accident had brought him to the spot at which he heard the uproar; but that *having* heard it, and connecting it with the khan's communication of the morning, he had then designedly gone after the sound in a way which he certainly should not have done at so critical a moment, unless in the expectation of finding the khan assaulted by assassins. A few minutes after, they reached the outpost at which it became safe to leave the Tartar chieftain; and immediately the four fugitives commenced a flight which is perhaps without a parallel in the annals of travelling. Each of them led six or seven horses besides the one he rode; and by shifting from one to the other (like the ancient *desultors* of the Roman circus), so as never to burden the same horse for more than half an hour at a time, they continued to advance at the rate of two hundred miles in the twenty-four hours for three days consecutively.

After that time, conceiving themselves beyond pursuit, they proceeded less rapidly, though still with a velocity which staggered the belief of Weseloff's friends in after years. He was, however, a man of high principle, and always adhered firmly to the details of his printed report. One of the circumstances there stated is, that they continued to pursue the route by which the Kalmucks had fled, never for an instant finding any difficulty in tracing it by the skeletons and other memorials of their calamities. In particular, he mentions vast heaps of money as part of the valuable property which it had been necessary to sacrifice. These heaps were found lying still untouched in the deserts. From these, Weseloff and his companions took as much as they could conveniently carry; and this it was, with the price of their beautiful horses (which they afterwards sold at one of the Russian military settlements for about fifteen pounds apiece), which eventually enabled them to pursue their journey in Russia. This journey, as regarded Weseloff in particular, was closed by a tragical catastrophe. He was at that time young, and the only child of a doting mother. Her affliction under the violent abduction of her son had been excessive, and probably had undermined her constitution. Still she had supported it. Weseloff, giving way to the natural impulses of his filial affection, had imprudently posted through Russia to his mother's house without warning of his approach. He rushed precipitately into her presence; and she, who had stood the shocks of sorrow, was found unequal to the shock of joy too sudden and too acute. She died upon the spot.

I now revert to the final scenes of the Kalmuck flight. These it would be useless to pursue circumstantially through the whole two thousand miles of suffering which remained; for the character of that suffering was even more monotonous than on the former half of the flight, and also more severe. Its main elements were excessive heat, with the accompaniments of famine and thirst, but aggravated at every step by the murderous attacks of their cruel enemies, the Bashkirs and the Kirghizes.

These people, "more fell than anguish, hunger, or the sea," stuck to the unhappy Kalmucks like a swarm of enraged hornets. And very often, whilst *they* were attacking them in the rear, their advanced parties and flanks were attacked with almost equal fury by the people of the country which they were traversing; and with good reason, since the law of self-preservation had now obliged the fugitive Tartars to plunder provisions and to forage wherever they passed. In this respect their condition was a constant oscillation of wretchedness: for sometimes, pressed by grinding famine, they took a circuit of perhaps a hundred miles in order to strike into a land rich in the comforts of life. But in such a land they were sure to find a crowded population, of which every arm was raised in unrelenting hostility, with all the advantages of local knowledge, and with constant preoccupation of all the defensible positions, mountain passes, or bridges. Sometimes, again, wearied out with this mode of suffering, they took a circuit of perhaps a hundred miles in order to strike into a land with few or no inhabitants; but in such a land they were sure to meet absolute starvation. Then, again, whether with or without this plague of starvation, whether with or without this plague of hostility in front, whatever might be the "fierce varieties" of their misery in this respect, no rest ever came to their unhappy rear; *post equitem sedet atra cura;* it was a torment like the undying worm of conscience, and upon the whole it presented a spectacle altogether unprecedented in the history of mankind. Private and personal malignity is not unfrequently immortal; but rare indeed is it to find the same pertinacity of malice in a nation. And what imbittered the interest was, that the malice was reciprocal. Thus far the parties met upon equal terms; but that equality only sharpened the sense of their dire inequality as to other circumstances. The Bashkirs were ready to fight "from morn to dewy eve." The Kalmucks, on the contrary, were always obliged to run. Was it *from* their enemies as creatures whom they feared? No, but *towards* their friends,— towards that final haven of China,— as what was hourly implored by their wives and the tears of their children. But, though they fled unwillingly, too often they fled in vain, being unwillingly recalled. There lay the torment. Every day the Bashkirs fell upon them; every day the same unprofitable battle was renewed. As a matter of course, the Kalmucks recalled part of their advanced guard to fight them. Every day the battle raged for hours, and uniformly with the same result; for, no sooner did the Bashkirs find themselves too heavily pressed, and that the Kalmuck march had been retarded by some hours, than they retired into the boundless deserts, where all pursuit was hopeless. But if the Kalmucks resolved to press forward, regardless of their enemies, in that case their attacks became so fierce and overwhelming that the general safety seemed likely to be brought into question; nor could any effectual remedy be applied to the case, even for each separate day, except by a most embarrassing halt and by countermarches that to men in their circumstances were almost worse than death. It will not be surprising that the irritation of such a systematic persecution, superadded to a previous and hereditary hatred, and accompanied by the stinging consciousness of utter impotence as regarded all effectual vengeance, should gradually have inflamed the Kalmuck animosity into the wildest expression of downright madness and frenzy. Indeed, long before the frontiers of China were approached, the hostility of both sides had assumed the appearance much more of a warfare amongst wild beasts than amongst creatures acknowledging the restraints of reason or the claims of a common nature. The spectacle became too atrocious: it was that of a host of lunatics pursued by a host of fiends.

On a fine morning in early autumn of the year 1771, Kien Long, the Emperor of China, was pursuing his amusements in a wild frontier district lying on the outside of the Great Wall. For many hundred square leagues the country was desolate of inhabitants, but rich in woods of ancient growth, and overrun with game of every description. In a central spot of this solitary region the emperor had built a gorgeous hunting lodge, to which he resorted annually for recreation, and relief from the cares of government. Led onwards in pursuit of game, he had rambled to a distance of two hundred miles or more from this lodge, followed at a little distance by a sufficient military escort, and every night pitching his tent in a different situation, until at length he had arrived on the very margin of the vast central deserts of Asia. Here he was standing, by accident, at an opening of his pavilion, enjoying the morning sunshine, when suddenly to the westward there arose a vast, cloudy vapor, which by degrees expanded, mounted, and seemed to be slowly diffusing itself over the whole face of the heavens. By and by this vast sheet of mist began to thicken towards the horizon, and to roll forward in billowy volumes. The emperor's suite assembled from all quarters; the silver trumpets were sounded in the rear; and from all the glades and forest avenues began to trot forward towards the pavilion the yagers — half cavalry, half huntsmen — who composed the imperial escort. Conjecture was on the stretch to divine the cause of this phenomenon; and the interest continually increased in proportion as simple curiosity gradually deepened into the anxiety of uncertain danger. At first it had been imagined that some vast troops of deer or other wild animals of the chase had been disturbed in their forest haunts by the emperor's movements, or possibly by wild beasts prowling for

prey, and might be fetching a compass by way of re-entering
the forest grounds at some remoter points secure from
molestation. But this conjecture was dissipated by the
slow increase of the cloud and the steadiness of its motion.
In the course of two hours the vast phenomenon had advanced to a point which was judged to be within five miles
of the spectators, though all calculations of distance were
difficult, and often fallacious, when applied to the endless
expanses of the Tartar deserts. Through the next hour,
during which the gentle morning breeze had a little fresh-
ened, the dusty vapor had developed itself far and wide into
the appearance of huge aërial draperies, hanging in mighty
volumes from the sky to the earth; and at particular points,
where the eddies of the breeze acted upon the pendulous
skirts of these aërial curtains, rents were perceived, sometimes taking the form of regular arches, portals, and windows,
through which began dimly to gleam the heads of camels
"indorsed" with human beings, and at intervals the moving of men and horses in tumultuous array, and then through
other openings, or vistas, at far-distant points, the flashing
of polished arms. But sometimes, as the wind slackened
or died away, all those openings, of whatever form, in the
cloudy pall, would slowly close, and for a time the whole
pageant was shut up from view; although the growing din,
the clamors, the shrieks and groans ascending from infuriated
myriads, reported, in a language not to be misunderstood,
what was going on behind the cloudy screen.

It was, in fact, the Kalmuck host, now in the last extremi-
ties of their exhaustion, and very fast approaching to that
final stage of privation and intense misery beyond which
few or none could have lived, but also, happily for themselves, fast approaching (in a literal sense) that final stage
of their long pilgrimage at which they would meet hospi-
tality on a scale of royal magnificence, and full protection
from their enemies. These enemies, however, as yet, still

were hanging on their rear as fiercely as ever, though this day was destined to be the last of their hideous persecution. The khan had, in fact, sent forward couriers with all the requisite statements and petitions, addressed to the Emperor of China. These had been duly received, and preparations made in consequence to welcome the Kalmucks with the most paternal benevolence. But as these couriers had been despatched from the Torgau at the moment of arrival thither, and before the advance of Traubenberg had made it necessary for the khan to order a hasty renewal of the flight, the emperor had not looked for their arrival on their frontier until full three months after the present time. The khan had, indeed, expressly notified his intention to pass the summer heats on the banks of the Torgau, and to recommence his retreat about the beginning of September. The subsequent change of plan, being unknown to Kien Long, left him for some time in doubt as to the true interpretation to be put upon this mighty apparition in the desert; but at length the savage clamors of hostile fury and the clangor of weapons unveiled to the emperor the true nature of those unexpected calamities which had so prematurely precipitated the Kalmuck measure.

Apprehending the real state of affairs, the emperor instantly perceived that the first act of his fatherly care for these erring children (as he esteemed them), now returning to their ancient obedience, must be to deliver them from their pursuers. And this was less difficult than might have been supposed. Not many miles in the rear was a body of well-appointed cavalry, with a strong detachment of artillery, who always attended the emperor's motions. These were hastily summoned. Meantime it occurred to the train of courtiers that some danger might arise to the emperor's person from the proximity of a lawless enemy; and accordingly he was induced to retire a little to the rear. It soon appeared, however, to those who watched the vapory shroud

in the desert, that its motion was not such as would argue
the direction of the march to be exactly upon the pavilion,
but rather in a diagonal line, making an angle of full forty-
five degrees with that line in which the imperial *cortège*
5 had been standing, and therefore with a distance continually
increasing. Those who knew the country judged that the
Kalmucks were making for a large fresh-water lake about
seven or eight miles distant. They were right; and to that
point the imperial cavalry was ordered up; and it was pre-
10 cisely in that spot, and about three hours after, and at noon-
day, on the 8th of September, that the great exodus of the
Kalmuck Tartars was brought to a final close, and with a
scene of such memorable and hellish fury as formed an appropriate winding up to an expedition in all its parts and
15 details so awfully disastrous. The emperor was not personally present, or at least he saw whatever he *did* see from
too great a distance to discriminate its individual features;
but he records in his written memorial the report made to
him of this scene by some of his own officers.

20 The Lake of Tengis, near the frightful Desert of Kobi,
lay in a hollow amongst hills of a moderate height, ranging
generally from two or three thousand feet high. About
eleven o'clock in the forenoon the Chinese cavalry reached
the summit of a road which led through a cradle-like dip in
25 the mountains right down upon the margin of the lake.
From this pass, elevated about two thousand feet above the
level of the water, they continued to descend, by a very
winding and difficult road, for an hour and a half; and during the whole of this descent they were compelled to be
30 inactive spectators of the fiendish spectacle below. The
Kalmucks, reduced by this time from about six hundred
thousand souls to two hundred thousand, and after enduring
for two months and a half the miseries we have previously
described,—outrageous heat, famine, and the destroying
35 scimitar of the Kirghizes and the Bashkirs,—had for the

last ten days been traversing a hideous desert, where no
vestiges were seen of vegetation, and no drop of water could
be found. Camels and men were already so overladen that
it was a mere impossibility that they should carry a toler-
able sufficiency for the passage of this frightful wilderness.
On the eighth day the wretched daily allowance, which had
been continually diminishing, failed entirely; and thus, for
two days of insupportable fatigue, the horrors of thirst had
been carried to the fiercest extremity. Upon this last morning, at the sight of the hills and the forest scenery, which
announced to those who acted as guides the neighborhood
of the Lake of Tengis, all the people rushed along with maddening eagerness to the anticipated solace. The day grew
hotter and hotter, the people more and more exhausted;
and gradually, in the general rush forwards to the lake, all
discipline and command were lost, all attempts to preserve
a rear-guard were neglected. The wild Bashkirs rode in
amongst the encumbered people, and slaughtered them by
wholesale and almost without resistance. Screams and
tumultuous shouts proclaimed the progress of the massacre;
but none heeded, none halted: all alike, pauper or noble,
continued to rush on with maniacal haste to the waters, —
all with faces blackened by the heat preying upon the liver,
and with tongue drooping from the mouth. The cruel Bashkir was affected by the same misery, and manifested the
same symptoms of his misery, as the wretched Kalmuck.
The murderer was oftentimes in the same frantic misery
as his murdered victim. Many, indeed (an ordinary effect
of thirst), in both nations, had become lunatic; and in this
state, whilst mere multitude and condensation of bodies
alone opposed any check to the destroying scimitar and
the trampling hoof, the lake was reached; and into that the
whole vast body of enemies rushed, and together continued
to rush, forgetful of all things at that moment but of one
almighty instinct. This absorption of the thoughts in one

maddening appetite lasted for a single minute; but in the next arose the final scene of parting vengeance. Far and wide the waters of the solitary lake were instantly dyed red with blood and gore. Here rode a party of savage Bashkirs, hewing off heads as fast as the swaths fall before the mower's scythe; there stood unarmed Kalmucks in a death grapple with their detested foes, both up to the middle in water, and oftentimes both sinking together below the surface, from weakness or from struggles, and perishing in each other's arms. Did the Bashkirs at any point collect into a cluster for the sake of giving impetus to the assault, thither were the camels driven in fiercely by those who rode them, generally women or boys; and even these quiet creatures were forced into a share in this carnival of murder by trampling down as many as they could strike prostrate with the lash of their fore-legs. Every moment the water grew more polluted; and yet every moment fresh myriads came up to the lake, and rushed in, not able to resist their frantic thirst, and swallowing large draughts of water visibly contaminated with the blood of their slaughtered compatriots. Wheresoever the lake was shallow enough to allow of men raising their heads above the water, there, for scores of acres, were to be seen all forms of ghastly fear, of agonizing struggle, of spasm, of convulsion, of mortal conflict, — death, and the fear of death; revenge, and the lunacy of revenge; hatred, and the frenzy of hatred; until the neutral spectators, of whom there were not a few, now descending the eastern side of the lake, at length averted their eyes in horror. This horror, which seemed incapable of further addition, was, however, increased by an unexpected incident. The Bashkirs, beginning to perceive here and there the approach of the Chinese cavalry, felt it prudent, wheresoever they were sufficiently at leisure from the passions of the murderous scene, to gather into bodies. This was noticed by the governor of a small Chinese fort built upon an eminence above the lake; and immediately he threw in a broadside, which spread havoc amongst the Bashkir tribe. As often as the Bashkirs collected into "*globes*" and "*turms*" as their only means of meeting the long line of descending Chinese cavalry, so often did the Chinese governor of the fort pour in his exterminating broadside; until at length the lake, at the lower end, became one vast seething caldron of human bloodshed and carnage. The Chinese cavalry had reached the foot of the hills; the Bashkirs, attentive to *their* movements, had formed; skirmishes had been fought; and with a quick sense that the contest was henceforward rapidly becoming hopeless, the Bashkirs and Kirghizes began to retire. The pursuit was not as vigorous as the Kalmuck hatred would have desired; but at the same time the very gloomiest hatred could not but find in their own dreadful experience of the Asiatic deserts, and in the certainty that these wretched Bashkirs had to repeat that same experience a second time, for thousands of miles, as the price exacted by a retributory Providence for their vindictive cruelty, — not the very gloomiest of the Kalmucks, or the least reflecting, but found in all this a retaliatory chastisement more complete and absolute than any which their swords and lances could have obtained, or human vengeance could have devised.

Here ends the tale of the Kalmuck wanderings in the desert; for any subsequent marches which awaited them were neither long nor painful. Every possible alleviation and refreshment for their exhausted bodies had been already provided by Kien Long with the most princely munificence; and lands of great fertility were immediately assigned to them in ample extent along the river Ily, not very far from the point at which they had first emerged from the wilderness of Kobi. But the beneficent attention of the Chinese emperor may be best stated in his own words, as translated into French by one of the Jesuit missionaries: "La nation des Torgotes (*savoir les Kalmuques*) arriva à Ily, toute delabrée, n'ayant ni de quoi vivre, ni de quoi se vêtir. Je l'avais prévu; et j'avais ordonné de faire en tout genre les provisions nécessaires pour pouvoir les secourir promptement; c'est ce qui a été exécuté. On a fait la division des terres: et on a assigné à chaque famille une portion suffisante pour pouvoir servir à son entretien, soit en la cultivant, soit en y nourissant des bestiaux. On a donné à chaque particulier des étoffes pour l'habiller, des grains pour se nourrir pendant l'espace d'une année, des ustensiles pour le ménage et d'autres choses nécessaires: et outre cela plusieurs onces d'argent, pour se pourvoir de ce qu'on aurait pu oublier. On a designé des lieux particuliers, fertiles en pâturages; et on leur a donné des bœufs, moutons, etc., pour qu'ils pussent dans la suite travailler par eux-mêmes à leur entretien et à leur bienêtre."

These are the words of the emperor himself, speaking in his own person of his own paternal cares; but another Chinese, treating the same subject, records the munificence of this prince in terms which proclaim still more forcibly the disinterested generosity which prompted, and the delicate considerateness which conducted, this extensive bounty. He has been speaking of the Kalmucks, and he goes on thus: "Lorsqu'ils arrivèrent sur nos frontières (au nombre de plusieurs centaines de mille, quoique la fatigue extrême, la faim, la soif, et toutes les autres incommodités inséparables d'une très-longue et très pénible route en eussent fait périr presque autant), ils étaient réduits à la dernière misère; ils manquaient de tout. Il [l'empereur, Kien Long] leur fit préparer des logemens conformes à leur manière de vivre; il leur fit distribuer des aliments et des habits; il leur fit donner des bœufs, des moutons, et des ustensiles, pour les mettre en état de former des troupeaux et de cultiver la terre, *et tout cela à ses propres frais*, qui se sont montés à des sommes immenses, sans compter l'argent qu'il a donné à chaque chef-de-famille, pour pourvoir à la subsistance de sa femme et de ses enfans."

Thus, after their memorable year of misery, the Kalmucks were replaced in territorial possessions, and in comfort equal perhaps, or even superior, to that which they had enjoyed in Russia, and with superior political advantages. But, if equal or superior, their condition was no longer the same: if not in degree, their social prosperity had altered in quality; for, instead of being a purely pastoral and vagrant people, they were now in circumstances which obliged them to become essentially dependent upon agriculture, and thus far raised in social rank, that, by the natural course of their habits and the necessities of life, they were effectually reclaimed from roving and from the savage customs connected with so unsettled a life. They gained also in political privileges, chiefly through the immunity from military service which their new relations enabled them to obtain. These were circumstances of advantage and gain. But one great disadvantage there was, amply to overbalance all other possible gain,—the chances were lost, or were removed to an incalculable distance, for their conversion to Christianity, without which in these times there is no absolute advance possible on the path of true civilization.

One word remains to be said upon the *personal* interests concerned in this great drama. The catastrophe in this respect was remarkable and complete. Oubacha, with all his goodness, and incapacity of suspecting, had, since the mysterious affair on the banks of the Torgau, felt his mind alienated from his cousin. He revolted from the man that would have murdered him; and he had displayed his caution so visibly as to provoke a reaction in the bearing of Zebek-Dorchi, and a displeasure which all his dissimulation could not hide. This had produced a feud, which, by keeping them aloof, had probably saved the life of Oubacha; for the friendship of Zebek-Dorchi was more fatal than his open enmity. After the settlement on the Ily, this feud continued to advance, until it came under the notice of the emperor on occasion of a visit which all the Tartar chieftains made to his Majesty at his hunting lodge in 1772. The emperor informed himself accurately of all the particulars connected with the transaction, of all the rights and claims put forward, and of the way in which they would severally affect the interests of the Kalmuck people. The consequence was, that he adopted the cause of Oubacha, and repressed the pretensions of Zebek-Dorchi, who, on his part, so deeply resented this discountenance to his ambitious projects, that, in conjunction with other chiefs, he had the presumption even to weave nets of treason against the emperor himself. Plots were laid, were detected, were baffled: counterplots were constructed upon the same basis and with the benefit of the opportunities thus offered.

Finally Zebek-Dorchi was invited to the imperial lodge, together with all his accomplices; and, under the skilful management of the Chinese nobles in the emperor's establishment, the murderous artifices of these Tartar chieftains were made to recoil upon themselves; and the whole of them perished by assassination at a great imperial banquet; for the Chinese morality is exactly of that kind which approves in everything the *lex talionis:* —

"Lex nec justior ulla est [as *they* think]
Quam necis artifices arte perire sua."

So perished Zebek-Dorchi, the author and originator of the great Tartar exodus. Oubacha, meantime, and his people were gradually recovering from the effects of their misery, and repairing their losses. Peace and prosperity, under the gentle rule of a fatherly lord paramount, redawned upon the tribes; their household *lares*, after so harsh a translation to distant climates, found again a happy reinstatement in what had, in fact, been their primitive abodes; they found themselves settled in quiet sylvan scenes, rich in all the luxuries of life, and endowed with the perfect loveliness of Arcadian beauty. But from the hills of this favored land, and even from the level grounds, as they approach its western border, they still look out upon that fearful wilderness which once beheld a nation in agony, — the utter extirpation of nearly half a million from amongst its numbers, and for the remainder a storm of misery so fierce that in the end (as happened also at Athens, during the Peloponnesian War, from a different form of misery) very many lost their memory; all records of their past life were wiped out as with a sponge, utterly erased and cancelled; and many others lost their reason, some in a gentle form of pensive melancholy, some in a more restless form of feverish delirium and nervous agitation, and others in the fixed forms of tempestuous mania, raving frenzy, or moping idiocy. Two great commemorative monuments arose in after years to mark the depth and permanence of the awe, the sacred and reverential grief, with which all persons looked back upon the dread calamities attached to the year of the *tiger*, — all who had either personally shared in those calamities and had themselves drunk from that cup of sorrow, or who had effectually been made witnesses to their results, and associated with their relief: two great monuments, we say: first of all, one in the religious solemnity, enjoined by the dalai-lama, called in the Tartar language a *Romanang;* that is, a national commemoration, with music the most rich and solemn, of all the souls who departed to the rest of paradise from the afflictions of the desert. This took place about six years after the arrival in China. Secondly, another, more durable, and more commensurate to the scale of the calamity and to the grandeur of this national exodus, in the mighty columns of granite and brass erected by the emperor, Kien Long, near the banks of the Ily. These columns stand upon the very margin of the steppes, and they bear a short but emphatic inscription to the following effect: —

By the will of God,
Here, upon the brink of these deserts,
Which from this point begin and stretch away,
Pathless, treeless, waterless,
For thousands of miles, and along the margins of many mighty nations,
Rested from their labors and from great afflictions,
Under the shadow of the Chinese Wall,
And by the favor of KIEN LONG, God's Lieutenant upon Earth,
The ancient Children of the Wilderness, — the Torgote Tartars, —
Flying before the wrath of the Grecian czar;
Wandering sheep who had strayed away from the Celestial Empire in the year 1616,
But are now mercifully gathered again, after infinite sorrow,
Into the fold of their forgiving shepherd.
Hallowed be the spot forever,
And hallowed be the day — September 8, 1771!
Amen.

NOTES.

An account of this singular flight of a Tartar tribe was written by the Chinese Emperor, as a state paper, in the Chinese language. Roman Catholic missionaries translated parts of it, but the paper itself was very long, and in it the Emperor gives the reasons for his own treatment of the Kalmucks.

Cambyses, king of the Medes and Persians, son of Cyrus, B.C. 529. Defeated Psammenitus, B.C. 525, and Egypt became a Persian province. The ruin of many of the monuments of Egypt is attributed to these invaders and their king, who was crazy.

Anabasis of Cyrus. Known to schoolboys as Xenophon's Anabasis. Cyrus was the son of Darius the Persian. At Cunaxa he was defeated by his brother and slain B.C. 401.

Crassus, Consul B.C. 55, was defeated by the Parthians with immense slaughter and put to death B.C. 53.

Julian, Roman Emperor, surnamed the Apostate, was killed, A.D. 363, in his expedition against the Persians.

Napoleon's retreat from Moscow, A.D. 1812.

For the "*great scriptural Exodus of the Israelites*," read the Book of Exodus, Old Testament.

The Huns. Nomadic Scythian tribes, who devastated the Roman Empire in the fifth century. They inhabited the plains of Tartary, near China. Attila was their great leader. The Hungarians are the descendants of the Huns.

Avars, or Avari. A Mongolian race, some of whom in the sixth century settled on the Danube. Conquered the Dalmatians and some German tribes. Were driven from Dalmatia A.D. 640.

Mongol Tartars. Nearly allied to the Mongol race. Brought under Mongolic sway by Genghis Khan in the twelfth century. Western Tartary belongs to Russia; Eastern Tartary to China. Tartary and Turkestan are, in a restricted sense, the same country.

War between Russia and Turkey was frequently renewed after Peter the Great, in 1711, was defeated but allowed to escape with his army. By the peace of 1774, Russia obtained a large accession of territory and the Black Sea.

The Bashkirs. A Tartar tribe of Russia, living principally in tents, except in winter. They are Mohammedans, and guard the frontiers of Russia. Their territory lies north of the Caspian Sea, on the rivers Volga and Ural and their branches.

Kirghizes. A Mongol race, on the southern frontier of Asiatic Russia, on barren plains abounding in salt lakes. They are often called the Cossacks of the Steppes.

The Cossacks. A mixed Caucasian and Tartar race. They are dashing light-horse troops and form a military cordon of the empire of the Czar, extending from the Black Sea nearly to the Sea of Okhotsk in Eastern Siberia.

Astrakhan. A part of European Russia, northwest of the Caspian Sea, divided by the river Volga into two nearly equal parts. The people on the Caspian have extensive fisheries, but the tribes are mostly nomadic.

Russia. An absolute monarchy. The Czar is the real head of the nation and of the Greco-Russian Church. When Peter the Great ascended the throne in 1696, the policy and destiny of Russia were immediately changed. From this period the policy of Russia has been to extend her dominions east and south. Under Catharine II. she acquired great possessions in Poland and on the Black Sea. Notwithstanding the Crimean war, which humbled for a time the military pride of Russia, that nation has continued to advance. It has become one of the most powerful, as well as one of the most extensive, nations of modern times. It has an immense army of regular troops, and a feudal militia of the Cossacks and similar races. It has become the ruler and, to some extent, the pacificator of the barbarous tribes of Turkestan. It has great political influence in Persia. It menaces the possessions of England in Asia, although Afghanistan is the independent "buffer" state between the two rival nations and holds the Gates of Herat, the key of the situation. Lately, by taking the part of China in negotiations with Japan, after the disastrous defeat upon the sea of the Chinese by the Japanese, Russia has gained a strong foothold in the Celestial Empire.

It is supposed to have, as its ultimate aim, the possession of Constantinople, and has already control of the Black and Caspian seas. The loss of a great Tartar tribe, therefore, in 1771, was humiliating to Russia's pride. Hence the pursuit and sanguinary attacks upon the fleeing Kalmucks.

NOTES. 81

The Kalmucks, or Calmucks, had been expelled from China in 1672, but had been repeatedly invited to return. The tribe of the Derbets, or Tchoros, west of the Volga, did not join in the flight, and their descendants remain still in that region. De Quincey's estimate of the number of Tartars, whose flight he records, must be greatly exaggerated, if other sources of information can be relied upon. Three hundred thousand souls would probably be nearer the fact. The distance traveled, which he speaks of incidentally as 4000 miles, could not have exceeded 2000 miles, counting in all deflections from a straight course; for the new Trans-Siberian railway, to be completed in 1905, and extending from European Russia, through Siberia and Manchuria, to the Japan Sea, is but 4741 miles long.

On the map, the route of the flight may be approximately traced by the dotted lines; the railway runs some hundreds of miles north. The student may profitably consult a large map of Central Asia for information concerning the boundaries of Russia in Asia at the present time. Russia's geographical relations with Turkey, Persia, Afghanistan, India, and China should also be studied.

At the present time there is another "Flight" eastward which reminds one of the Kalmuck migration a century ago. It is a wild stampede of emigration, at first encouraged by the government, and which it now in vain endeavors to check. In 1894, 180,000 peasants set out for Siberia. Between the months of January and May, 1896, 170,000 people had already passed on, and in May alone 100,000. Transportation lines are choked, with all the attendant miseries of hunger, despair, and death. Thus history repeats itself as civilization advances and the centuries roll on.

Jaik River (p. 46). Now called the Ural.

Wolga River (p. 46). Same as the Volga.

"Trashed" (p. 51, 5th line), means encumbered by indispensable baggage.

"Indorsed" (p. 68, 18th line), from *in* and *dorsum* — with "human beings" on the camels' backs.

The inscription at end of text has been changed from Chinese symbols of dates, to coincide with the Christian era.

The term "Grecian czar" may have been used because the Russian Czar was supposed to be the successor of the Byzantine Cæsars, being of the same faith with them; or, simply because the faith of the Russian Czar and of the Russian Church was Greek.

www.ingramcontent.com/pod-product-compliance
Lightning Source LLC
Chambersburg PA
CBHW020729100426
42735CB00038B/1383